D0501549

DATE DUE

AP24'0			

Birdwatching
A Guide for Beginners

JOAN EASTON LENTZ & JUDITH YOUNG

Illustrated by Karen Foster

CAPRA PRESS
Santa Barbara

WE gratefully acknowledge the inspiration of Chuck Bernstein and the expert assistance of Larry Ballard, Louis Bevier, Karen Bridgers, Jon Dunn, Paul Lehman and T. Dion Warren. We would also like to thank our families for their patience and encouragement.

Cover and illustrations by Karen Foster.
Typography by Cook/Sundstrom Associates.

LIBRARY OF CONGRESS CATALOGUING IN PUBLICATION DATA
Lentz, Joan, 1942-
Birdwatching: a guide for beginners.
Bibliography: p.
1. Birdwatching.   I. Young, Judith, 1940-
II. Title.
QL677.5.L45   1985   598'.07'234   84-23676
ISBN 0-88496-231-8 (pbk.)

CAPRA PRESS
Post Office Box 2068
Santa Barbara, CA 93120

Contents

Introduction

ABOUT THIS BOOK

Birdwatching is largely taught as an oral tradition. Despite hundreds of books written about birds, their habitats and life cycles, the art of field identification has been chiefly passed from person to person. And this is still a good way to learn. However, getting started in birdwatching can be daunting! There are so many different species of birds, and some of the subtleties of identification take years, and much travel, to learn. We feel the beginning techniques can easily be mastered from a book.

In *Birdwatching: A Guide for Beginners* we give you an introductory class in birdwatching and provide tips that will make your birding trips more successful and fun. Birding becomes more exciting the more you understand. If you know what birds live in your local habitat, and if you grasp some of the factors influencing their behavior, you will know which birds to look for. And, you will be much more accurate in your identifications!

Birdwatching: A Guide for Beginners is more than a field guide. It attempts to make sense of the multiplicity of birds found in North America and gives you instructions on how to observe and record your sightings. This volume will show you how birds are classified, why they behave the way they do, and how you can make correct field identifications. You will learn all the

7

basic facts about birdwatching, plus gain an idea of which birds you are likely to encounter in a variety of habitats.

Birding is the fastest-growing sport in the United States today because it is exciting, adventuresome and takes us out of our largely manmade environments. Whether you live in the countryside or deep in the city, you can see hundreds of wild birds living out their daily dramas of survival. With small outlays of cash for equipment and with your own natural skills of observation heightened by interest and study, you can become expert in identifying and understanding the birds in your area.

As a sport, birdwatching is a community activity. We all rely on techniques and insights developed over generations by patient observers. Local hotlines, clubs and societies exist to help the amateur. With this support you will find your interest growing as much as your free time will allow. We hope *Birdwatching: A Guide for Beginners* will provide the impetus to involve you in a lifetime of successful birding. Welcome to the worldwide community of birders!

WHAT IS BIRDING?

What is birding? A sport? A hobby? A pastime? A career? Is it for the energetic mountain climber, or the serious librarian? Do you become involved with birding to meet people with similar interests or to study wildlife? Are you trying to escape the daily hassles of modern life, or do you want to learn more about nature?

Birding is the wet smell of fog in the air at 6:00 A.M. as you pull on your waders and walk out in the mud to study shorebirds. It is the excitement of identifying a new humming-bird whizzing by your feeder. It is the thrill of glimpsing the brilliant Western Tanager in the High Sierras. Birding is the immediacy of the chase when a rare bird stops off in town and the hotline is buzzing. Birding is watching the ducks and geese as they congregate in cold winter valleys. It is also the embarrassment of missing a new bird in the field when everyone else manages to find it. Birding can be the passion of a lifetime, or the whim of a Saturday morning when you go on your first birdwalk.

Birding is all of the above, and any other definitions you may want to invent. The actual term, birding, evolved from the more traditional word birdwatching. We use the terms interchangeably in this book, as do most birders today. And, we define it as the informal study of wild birds and their behavior in the field, usually by an amateur rather than an ornithologist. Many people think of it as a sport; and this may be the aspect that intrigues you. Earlier in the history of birdwatching, during the past century, amateur naturalists would collect specimens of as many bird species (and their eggs) as their ambitions and travels would allow. Nowadays, specimen collecting is rarely conducted, even by museums. The balance of wildlife in many modern habitats is too fragile to be tampered with in this way. Now birders collect birds on lists, in their notes, on film and in their memories.

Birdwatching can be pursued at any stage of life. For young people, it is a challenging introduction to the outdoors. Most of America's eminent ornithologists and naturalists had an unquenchable curiosity about birds in their childhood. As adults, when we are involved in making a living, birding can touch our lives as a weekend pursuit in the garden, on a walk, sailing or playing golf. Often one incident will spark our interest and spur our study of birds. The sight of a fabulously colorful grosbeak at the feeder, a Rufous-sided Towhee near the patio, a thrush that stuns itself while flying into the dining room window—any of these could be the impetus for a hobby that will ultimately change our lives. Later, when old age slows us down and calmer pursuits beckon, nothing is more rewarding than the study of birds at the backyard feeder, in a simple birdbath or foraging on the lawn.

Birdwatching will enrich every experience, from a walk to the mailbox to a journey of a thousand miles. Most of all, birding is a newly heightened awareness, as you open your senses and your mind to the natural world, and finally begin to notice what is really out there. Yes, it's been there all along! Those huge blue herons and great white egrets and lemon-tinged warblers and funny-looking woodpeckers are waiting for you. Come with us and discover this world.

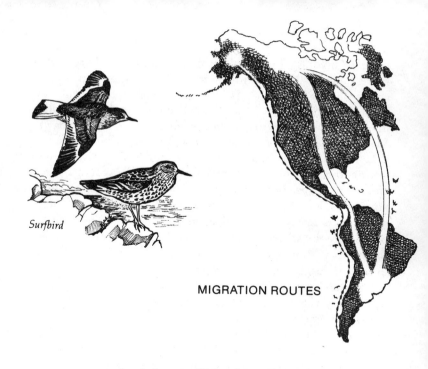

Surfbird

MIGRATION ROUTES

1. How Birds Live

THE ORIGIN OF BIRDS

The study of evolution is a painstaking and slow process. It takes generations to first discover and then piece together diverse bits of information from all over the globe. Charles Darwin first published his theory of evolution in 1859, and since then scientists have been corroborating his insights through the study of fossils and living species. However, in today's fast-paced electronic world it sometimes seems as if definitive answers on the origin of species will take as long to find as the process of evolution itself. It is unlikely the amateur naturalist or birdwatcher will be involved in the study of evolution, but the story of the development of birds provides provocative clues to a mystery we contemplate but may never completely understand.

The oldest bird fossil has been dated from about 150 million years ago. It was found in a limestone quarry in Germany and has been the source of much speculation. It was clearly a bird,

Lesser Golden-Plover

because the ancient stone bore the imprints of feathers growing from the forelimbs. But, the fossil was also strangely reptilian with a long tail, claws and separate teeth in both the upper and lower jaws. Apparently it had evolved from a line of small dinosaurs.

It is strange to think the long extinct dinosaurs are still represented on this planet by such a successful and diverse group as the birds. To the popular mind there is an obvious relationship between present day reptiles and those ancient monsters lumbering through the mud of our primeval swamps. Birds, however, have long been linked in men's minds with more fanciful and ethereal creatures, probably because of their facility in flight. In countless myths and folklore, birds have been associated with angels and other sacred dieties living in the heavens. But we can easily see their relationship to reptiles by looking at their legs and feet which still wear the same horny scales that covered the dinosaurs.

However, it is the presence of feathers that distinguishes birds as a group from all other animals; and it is the feathers that have tantalized many evolutionary theorists. In contrast to all contemporary reptiles and, probably, most dinosaurs, birds are warm-blooded. Was the feather an adaptation to conserve body heat or to facilitate flight? Scientists feel this ancient bird was probably a poor flier since it lacked the hollow bones and characteristic keel-shaped breast bone of modern birds. But no one knows which came first: feathers or flight?

Fossil records are sketchy, of course, but scientists think all bird species in existence now had evolved by the Pliocene epoch, between about two and five million years ago. Since then, the number of species seems to have diminished due to large climate changes, mountain building and, more recently, the effects of man's development on the environment. La Brea tar pits in Los Angeles is the site of the largest number of fossilized bird bones yet found. These fossils are of fairly recent origin, dating back about two million years, and are still being analyzed. Hopefully, more insights on the evolution of birds will come from this tarred treasure of bones.

DISTRIBUTION

No one knows how many different species of birds live on the planet today, but estimates we have read vary between 8,500 and 9,000. Almost every environment on earth supports some bird life, maybe not year-round but at least during the fertile season (e.g., the northern tundra and the arctic seas). The largest number of species occurs in the South American tropics. Here an enormous annual rainfall encourages the growth of tropical forests filled with a huge variety of plant and animal life. The Andes mountain range, rising from a tropical floor, provides many different subclimates and life zones promoting the kind of specialization that leads to the development of many distinct species. The continental United States, on the other hand, is populated by relatively few bird species, probably only around 650 species breed here regularly. In North America, though, you can find tremendously large concentrations of individual species in one place.

To study bird distribution, scientists have considered the full geographical range that each bird inhabits. Some birds live in the same area year-round, but many have separate breeding and wintering grounds and make bi-annual migrations back and forth between these sites. Many birds we see in this country during part of the year are really not local. They may winter here, or breed here or just pass through; many of them are on their way to or from Central and South America. The ability to fly has given birds so much mobility they are able to live much less restricted lives than most other animals. Probably only the great whales, moving unimpeded in the open ocean, migrate as much as birds. Scientists have tracked migration routes and tried to correlate them with changes in climate and geology over tens of thousands of years. In North America most migration is northward in the spring for breeding, and then southward again after nesting is completed.

Not only weather patterns, but the shapes and positions of the continents have changed over the millions of years birds have been on this planet. No one knows where birds first originated, or precisely how they have radiated out to occupy their present ranges. The question is: why migrate at all? Apparently migration provides a tremendous survival advantage. The fact that bird movements are seasonal and seem related to annual climate changes, leads scientists to believe migration is in response to the availability of food. When weather becomes severe the plants and insects in the affected area begin to die; then, birds will move to another area that will meet their needs. They may move only a short distance up a mountain, or they may cross a continent or the ocean. It would be wonderful if we could take the present ranges of bird habitation and work backwards to deduce where they originated and what drove them to develop their current migration routes and ranges. But this is a very complex task. Certainly the fairly recent periods of glaciation during the Ice Age affected the patterns of bird distribution. However, scientists feel many patterns of range and migration are much more ancient and reach back over a million years.

The origin of separate species may never be known, although ornithologists have reached some interesting conclusions by studying the families of birds rather than smaller categories, or species. They have assumed that if a family of birds exists in only one part of the world, it may have originated there. For instance, hummingbirds live only in the New World, and turkeys have inhabited only North America. By dividing the world into six large zoological regions that

each support similar life forms, scientists are slowly developing
a picture of where some bird families originated and how they
have managed to adapt to new regions. There is evidence the
Bering Sea was once covered by a land bridge connecting what
is now Siberia and Alaska, thereby allowing many animals to
range over both continents. Australia, however, seems to have
been isolated for so long that distinctly separate types of
birdlife have evolved there. No doubt the distribution of
contemporary bird families is changing right now in response
to many factors, including changes in climate and man's
development of the planet.

Birdwatchers become sensitive to distribution very quickly.
It is a great achievement in the birding world to spot a bird out
of its normal range. For instance, occasionally a migratory bird
from Siberia will start out with its internal compass turned
180 degrees. Instead of migrating down the coast of Asia, it
will move down the coast of North America where hundreds
of birders and dozens of hotlines will herald its arrival. Finding
a bird in a wrong spot—they are called rare birds or "accidentals"—is exciting, especially if you know what its normal
range is supposed to be. Field guides will give you a rough idea
of the breeding and wintering ranges of your local birds, and
checklists will narrow the distribution down to specific creek-
banks, National Parks, mountain tops, etc. To learn how to
assist in keeping track of everchanging ranges you should read
the sections in Chapter Seven "Taking Notes" and "The
Christmas Bird Count."

WHAT IS A BIRD?

Of all wildlife, birds are the most commonly studied and the easiest to observe. As a beginning birdwatcher you should know something about the physiology and habits of these melodious animals. Don't worry, you don't have to be an ornithologist to comprehend much about the life of birds. Your deeper understanding not only will help you learn the bird species, but will also heighten your enthusiasm as you set off on a field trip to glimpse a fragment of the lives of these aerial acrobats.

The ability to fly is the characteristic that has most astonished and intrigued men. Although bats and insects fly too, they are never viewed as such exotic engineers of flight as birds. What has allowed birds to take freely to the air and move, as a group, over almost the entire surface of the planet? The feather is the most obvious contribution to the gift of flight. When handling a feather we are impressed by its lightness, strength and flexibility. The shaft of the feather provides stiff support while the edges are soft and supple. Flight involves more than just an upward and downward motion of the wings, the leading feathers also must move forward and backward. Without the elastic strength of the feather, birds couldn't accomplish this motion. Feathers are also wonderful insulating material and can keep the birds warm, cool or dry. By fluffing up their feathers, birds can capture air next to their skin and provide an extra layer of warmth on cold nights. Water birds preen oil from specialized glands into their feathers so they can better float and swim on the water. Feathers are so important to birds that they have developed a system for renewing them after they have been worn for a while.

The process of changing feathers is called molt. When nestlings hatch from the egg some are naked and some already wear a covering of soft feathers called down. After a while these feathers are replaced with a juvenile coat which lasts until the bird is an adult. Each species of bird has its own pattern of molting, but most adult birds molt twice a year: in spring before mating, and in fall when the bird goes back to its winter plumage. Different authorities have assigned different names to the various molts, and reading these discussions can be very confusing. We have tried to simplify this and you can read a brief overview of molt in Chapter Three under "Plumage." The problem is: not all birds follow the same sequence of molts and some may molt as many as four times a year. The main point, though, is that during at least one molt all the feathers are replaced on the bird. Molting and feather regrowth require a big expenditure of energy, and in some cases (like the ducks) can render a bird flightless for a time. Most birds become secretive and quiet during a major molt. Apparently this risk must be taken because feathers are so crucial to the lifestyle of birds that they must be replaced annually.

What kind of animals wear these feathers? On the inside birds are very specialized creatures. Their skeleton is admirably adapted for flight. Their necks are long, with many more vertebrae than we possess. This enables them to maneuver well with their individualized bills and provides their head with much mobility during flight. Their breast bones have a pronounced keel for the attachment of the large flight muscles. Part of their skeletal system is fused together to provide a rigid undercarriage during flight. The bones are slender and hollow to cut down on the weight a bird has to carry.

Each species of bird has adapted the ability to fly to its own requirements and birds have come up with a variety of ways of moving through the air. Hummingbirds can beat their wings fifty or sixty times a second, whereas the albatross can glide and soar on wind currents over the ocean for hours without a single flap of its wings. As you become familiar with bird families, you will soon see marked differences in flight patterns.

Specialization for survival is not only illustrated by bird flight, it characterizes much of a bird's anatomy and behavior.

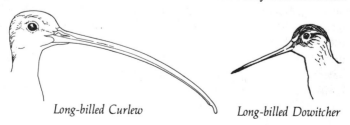

Long-billed Curlew   *Long-billed Dowitcher*

Because of this specialization, many different species of birds are able to occur together in an environment without direct competition. Bill shape is a clear example of specialization. Shorebirds all have probing bills for digging in mudflats and sand. But each bill is slightly different, some curve up while others curve down, and some are small and pointed while others are broad. The tiny, pointed bill of the sanderling is perfect for snatching crustaceans from the wet sand in the wake of retreating waves, while the longer, sturdy bill of the dowitcher is used to probe more deeply for creatures beneath the mud's surface. There is no 100 percent perfect correlation between bill shape and size and the lifestyle of birds, though the relationship is so pronounced that we often identify whole families of birds just by looking at their heads. Of course, bills serve the birds in more than food gathering. They are also important in defense and nest building.

Experienced birdwatchers will point out that bird feet also show obvious specialization. Birds use their feet to support them, to help them move, in nest building and to help procure their food. Webbed and lobed feet are important in swimming; the predator's taloned claws are used to capture and kill prey; the perching birds have feet with three toes forward and one pointing backward that lock when the bird settles on a branch; woodpeckers have two toes pointing forward and two pointing backward tipped with pointed claws to help them grasp the side of a tree trunk.

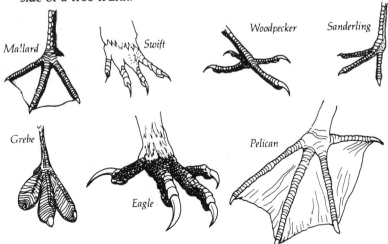

Mallard

Swift

Woodpecker

Sanderling

Grebe

Eagle

Pelican

Usually when you are birdwatching, you will observe the birds feeding or hunting for food. But in spring and summer a whole new set of behaviors can be seen; these revolve around reproduction and raising the young—the breeding cycle. This cycle is timed to take place when there is a maximum availability of food. Breeding behaviors vary with each species of bird and it is difficult to generalize for all of them. However, almost all birds begin their breeding cycle by establishing a territory. They will defend this territory from other kinds of birds, especially against those of their own species. It varies whether the territory is defended by the males, females or both. The territory is established in a healthy nesting spot with plenty of food available. Singing is probably the most commonly observed behavior in defense of territory. Although many poets would have you believe bird song is a romantic expression of pair bonding, in reality it is defensive/aggressive and the sites the bird sings from help delimit its territory. A variety of other aggressive behaviors will also mark territory. Territorial behaviors may help attract a mate, and later on in the season can develop into courtship behavior or rituals. The selection of a breeding territory and its defense obviously will maximize the chances of successfully raising the young by preventing competition for the same nesting spots and the same food sources.

Courtship rituals can become quite complex. Most are visual displays by the male that serve to trigger acceptance by the female. Ornithologists theorize that courtship displays in any animal help the members of a species identify each other and thereby prevent mating between species. Some birds do mate with the wrong species and occasionally this will result in hybrid offspring. But the chances of producing fertile eggs and healthy offspring are much greater within species than between species. Often the birds assume clearcut sex differences during courtship with the males showing much more aggressive behavior and the females demonstrating obvious submission.

The successful establishment of territory and attraction of a mate leads to copulation when the males fertilize the females. Around this time, nest building is usually started, although some birds may copulate only once and some during the entire nest building period. Nest building, too, is highly varied, but it serves the purpose of providing a protected place to brood the eggs and rear the young. Some birds are amazing architects, building beautifully complicated nests based on instinctual patterns. The actual nest designs and nesting behaviors (such as laying an egg in another bird's nest or using an old nest from the year before) are species specific. Hummingbirds build characteristic nests, and so do all other nest building birds. The nesting materials depend on what is available in the area. The typical cup nests of the songbirds have been found to contain an amazing variety of natural and manmade materials including such things as string, fishline, paper, fabric, yarn and even Christmas tinsel. The natural material gathered from the environment can include mud, plant materials, animal hairs and spider silk.

Egg laying varies by species, too. Some birds lay only one egg, some lay at least twenty in each clutch. Some birds will lay only one batch of eggs a year, some will lay several. Besides varying by species, egg laying depends on availability of food supply and various environmental factors, such as weather. Egg laying and the rearing of the young are so variable we won't try to summarize them here. But, it is entrancing behavior to observe, and you are lucky if you can spot a nest in your yard and watch the rearing of the young.

Birds in captivity live many times longer than wild birds. Scientists studying banded birds can calculate the age of individual birds; from this information they have estimated age limits for species. Not surprisingly, most birds die when they are young. The hazards are much greater during the first year of their life. Some estimates of mortality in the first year are as high as 75 percent. If they survive this period they may live for several more years but it is doubtful they will ever reach the advanced ages of caged birds. The relatively short life of wild birds concerns birdwatchers, but breeding strategies continue to produce enough birds to keep most contemporary species well represented in our habitats. If you become curious about the populations of birds in your area, you can create some interesting projects to study them.

2. Equipment Needed

One of the delights of birdwatching is the relative lack of equipment necessary. Shunning fancy clothes and expensive gear, most birders are satisfied to don a warm jacket, grab a pair of binoculars and a field guide, and venture out unencumbered by the costly accoutrements of other outdoor activities. Still, you should consider carefully which binoculars and field guide to purchase since you want your hours spent finding birds to yield maximum enjoyment. You may also want to listen to a few records in order to improve your knowledge of bird songs.

This chapter will cover the basic equipment needed to get started in birdwatching. In the beginning, the range of choices can be confusing. However, with a little help you can choose the equipment you need to set out on a satisfying lifetime of watching birds.

BINOCULARS AND SCOPES

For birdwatchers and naturalists, binoculars are indispensable tools for exploring the natural world. The optical principles governing binoculars derive from the simple laws of light refraction, first enunciated by Galileo. The first telescope, consisting of only two lenses, was invented by Galileo in 1609 and is still being used. Modern refinements have contributed to the expanding popularity and usefulness of binoculars, with over two million now sold annually in the United States.

Since World War II, binoculars have assumed a full range of shapes and sizes, far from the old-style field glasses which were, in fact, a pair of small Galilean telescopes. The first improvement was the Porro-prism binocular containing two prisms in each barrel, causing the path of light to zig-zag or fold upon itself. This shortens the space between the lens further from the eye (the objective lens) and the eyepiece, and thereby shortens the necessary length of the barrel. Even more advanced are the smaller and more elegant roof-prism binoculars which appeared on the market in the 1960s. These are usually in an H-shape, and are more expensive than Porro-prism binoculars.

All prismatic binoculars employ the same basic optical system: an objective lens (aimed at the object), a set of prisms, field lenses, and an ocular lens (eyepiece). In discussing the relative merits of different pairs of binoculars, an understanding of magnification, brilliance, resolution, field of view and alignment will assist you in your final decision.

Magnification, or power, means the number of times the object viewed is larger than when seen with the naked eye. You will see such figures as "7x35" stamped on the binoculars. The first figure refers to the magnification, and indicates the binocular magnifies seven times. The second figure indicates the diameter (in millimeters) of the objective lens. Some common power/size combinations are 7x35, 8x20, 8x30, 8x40, 10x40 and 10x50.

Magnification alone may not make detail more discernible, because the binoculars will magnify hand tremor as well as the object in the lens. Until recently, a magnification of seven was considered best for birders. However, birdwatchers often find an eight-power binocular works well in the field. Ten-power binoculars are also increasing in popularity due to their new roof-prism design, light weight and the birdwatcher's need to study small details from a distance. If you purchase ten-power binoculars, it is a good idea to have them close-focused at the factory. This will enable you to use them at a closer range than they would normally be effective. Many optical equipment companies provide close-focusing for a small additional fee when you purchase a pair.

Binoculars must be brilliant as well as powerful. The higher the magnification, the more light required to brighten the image. If you divide the diameter of the objective lens by the power of the binocular, you get the diameter of the exit pupil. This is simply a fancy way of measuring the amount of light reaching your eye. For instance, a 7x35 binocular would have an exit pupil of five millimeters. Binoculars for all-round daylight use are made with exit pupils ranging from three to five millimeters. Birdwatchers and naturalists choose a balance between power and brilliance, while wanting a lightweight binocular. The best formulas for this combination are 7x35, 8x40 and 10x40.

Resolution, or clarity, is determined by the optical system of the binoculars. Precision lenses are tested to demanding standards, and this is where the more expensive binoculars excel. Low-priced binoculars may cause headaches or eyestrain, as your eyes try to correct for inadequacies in the lenses.

The area that can be seen through a binocular at a given distance is its field of view. This is expressed in feet at 1,000 yards, or in degrees. A wide field of view is undesirable in cheap binoculars, and it makes good binoculars even more expensive.

When your binoculars are aligned perfectly, you see a single image with both eyes. Sometimes the prisms get out of position, or the frame becomes twisted so you see overlapping images. Eyestrain is the result, to be remedied by a good repairman or photographic supply store. Well-made binoculars will retain their alignment through the wear and tear of birding much better than an inferior pair.

Good binoculars are essential to your birdwatching. It simply will not suffice for you to pick up Aunt Jane's opera glasses or borrow an old pair of World War I field glasses. They can get you started, but you should research the purchase of a new pair of binoculars as soon as possible. There are many fine binoculars on the market at a variety of prices. The following manufacturers sell excellent products: Bushnell, Minolta,

Nikon, Pentax, Leitz, Swift and Zeiss. Our recommendation is to get the best possible pair you can afford from a reputable manufacturer. You will never regret it.

Once you have obtained your binoculars, you need to learn how to focus them. They can be focused in one of two ways, depending upon the model. The individual-focus binocular provides separate spiral adjustments on each eyepiece. These adjustments allow you to focus each eye separately.

However, most models have a center focus operated by a mechanism between the two barrels which brings both eye pieces to the same focal setting simultaneously. These binoculars are also equipped with an individual diopter focus on one of the eyepieces (usually the right one). Closing your right eye, use the center focus until the image seen by the left eye is clear. Then use the diopter adjustment to adjust the focus for the right eye. Once corrected for individual differences between your eyes, you need only use the center focus to obtain a clear image for both eyes. With one hand you can rapidly focus the binoculars. One popular type of center focus uses a lever mechanism instead of the center knob; it is called "Insta-Focus" and provides speedy focusing.

Birders who wear glasses have more difficulty looking through binoculars because the glasses form a barrier between the eyes and the lens, in effect narrowing your field of vision. Many manufacturers have added retractable eyecup attachments allowing your eyes to get closer to the lens, even if you wear glasses. Some birders lift their glasses when looking through their binoculars. You will have to experiment to find which is easier for you, and which provides the best view of the birds.

Spotting scopes can be considered an optional addition to your equipment. However, if you become serious about birdwatching you will undoubtedly want to purchase one. For shorebirds on mudflats far away, for hawk watching and for scrutinizing distant land birds, you really require a scope.

A scope brings birds from fifteen to sixty times closer, much closer than even the most powerful binoculars. Most scopes are long and fairly heavy, so they need a tripod for support. The tripod is a separate purchase. Using a scope takes practice, because you see a narrower field of vision than through your binoculars. Locating the bird in question with binoculars first aids in finding it through the scope.

There are two kinds of scopes: the refractive and the reflective. Refractive scopes are most commonly used by birders because they are much lower-priced. Refractive scopes usually come with a zoom capability, which alters the magnification with a twist of a dial. In seconds you can zoom from fifteen-power to forty-power. In the field, you will find it best to position the bird in your scope on the lowest magnification before zooming in with the higher power. With higher power settings, the image often gets distorted at the edge of the field of view. Currently, Bushnell manufactures a scope with interchangeable, fixed focal length eyepieces, of which the twenty-power and twenty-two-power wide angle are the most popular with birders. A scope is an invaluable tool for looking at waterfowl on lakes, scanning the ocean from shore for pelagic birds, studying resting gulls for field marks and numerous other birdwatching tasks.

The reflective scope employs the same principles as high-power astronomy telescopes. Incoming light rays are folded twice, by two mirrors, before reaching your eyes. Therefore, the length of the scope is less. Depending upon the eyepiece you use, reflective scopes can magnify from 20 to 250 times. These marvelous instruments are amazingly effective at bringing the birds up close, but are very expensive. They are often used on professional bird tours.

Purchasing a good, steady tripod for your scope is important. The least vibration from the wind or an accidental bump will blur your view. Seek a good balance between a tripod that is not too heavy to lug around, and yet one that is steady enough to anchor the scope to the ground. Most birders prefer a tripod with legs that lock into place with the flip of a small clamp, rather than the more time consuming variety that screw tight at each joint. Do not be discouraged if managing your scope and tripod seems ungainly at first . The ability to quickly set up and collapse a scope comes with time and frequent use.

FIELD GUIDES AND CHECKLISTS

Field guides and checklists are invaluable tools to bird identification. You will need to purchase a field guide to North
American birds before you continue further in birding. Use a
field guide to confirm your own observations, and to enhance
your knowledge of individual birds. The written descriptions
will include some behavior characteristics, and perhaps some
phonetic translations of typical bird calls. Most field guides will
have range maps, showing you where the birds winter and
breed. An understanding of the normal range of the birds will
help you find them in season and will alert you to rarities in
your neighborhood. The pictures in the field guide, whether
photographs or drawings, will help you remember the bird
visually long after it has flown away.

Never before has there been a more opportune time to take
up the study of birds. Why? The field guides available today
are excellent. Within the last twenty years the advancements
in field identification, along with the increased interest of
millions of American birdwatchers, has resulted in the publication of very sophisticated and accurate field guides. We
include a brief discussion of current guides. The bibliography
in the Appendix contains full publishing data on the books that
follow.

Roger Tory Peterson remains unchallenged as the pioneer
of the modern field guide. His three books contain the famous
Peterson system of arrows to point out key field marks on his
illustrations. This helpful technique alerts you at once to
plumage variations. Bird descriptions in the text are lengthier
than some guides and provide pertinent information on bird
calls and behavior. The newly-revised *A Field Guide to the Birds
(East of the Rockies)* has remedied one of the disadvantages of
these books—the separation between bird pictures and descriptions. The eastern guide also includes range maps, but they are
at the rear of the book, removed from the bird plates. *A Field
Guide to Western Birds* and *A Field Guide to the Birds of Texas* lack
range maps, preferring to state distribution in the text.
Although not as up-to-date as some other guides, these books
are excellent, especially on bird behavior. They are classics and

you will probably want all three if you travel in the United States.

Robbins, Bruun and Zim have written a single volume covering all of North America, *Birds of North America*. Published by Western under their Golden imprint, it is dubbed "the Golden guide" by most birders. This handy book first came out in 1966, and revolutionized the field guide concept. At last, publishers had succeeded in fitting the text opposite the bird's picture. No more flipping through plates and then searching elsewhere for the descriptive passage. However, bird descriptions had to be short to fit this format. In 1983, this book was revised and up-dated. Unfortunately, there are still minor inaccuracies in both the text and the illustrations, and the latter seem to have suffered in reprint. This book is low-priced, represents all of North America in one small volume, and is easy to use.

In 1983 the National Geographic Society published the beautiful *Field Guide to the Birds of North America*. High-quality paper and binding, well-executed illustrations and the accuracy of the text make this guide superb. Illustrations and text face each other, making it easy to use. The latest information on identification in the field has been included especially on plumage details. However, due to space considerations, some descriptions give little information on calls and behavior. Although this guide is largely unavailable in book stores, you can obtain one directly from the National Geographic Society. It is also stocked by some museums, Audubon societies and certain birdwatching catalogs.

A three-volume set of guides edited by John Farrand, *The Audubon Society Master Guide to Birding*, was published in 1983. You may want to wait until you have been birding awhile before you purchase this set packed with wonderful photos and in-depth coverage of each bird species. This is a very up-to-date publication written by current experts in field identification. However, its size is a drawback and some of the photos have been mislabeled and a few are poor representations. Each species has a page or more to itself. The wealth of material in these volumes might be intimidating to a beginner, but you will want to buy them as a reference tool later on.

As you become involved with birdwatching, you may wish

to collect older field guides. Some, although published years ago, are still attractive and surprisingly accurate. Early editions of all the Peterson guides are of great interest. In the 1950s three guides written by Richard Pough were published: *The Audubon Society Guide to Eastern Landbirds, The Audubon Society Guide to Waterbirds,* and *The Audubon Society Western Bird Guide* are well worth acquiring for their charming paintings and lengthy accounts. Going back still further, especially if you are interested in western birds, get a copy of Ralph Hoffmann's *Birds of the Pacific States* published in 1927. It is fascinating reading and the descriptions of bird songs and calls are excellent. Easterners will want to turn the pages of another old-fashioned but immensely informative handbook, *Birds of Eastern North America* by Frank M. Chapman, 1930.

You can search for these books in used-book stores and garage sales. They are worth the time you spend hunting for them. Remember, though, the birds will be classified by an older system and may have unfamiliar common names or family designations. These forgotten treasures, written in a more leisurely era, often contain interesting facts that modern guidebooks have neither the time nor space to handle.

Checklists are simple listings of bird species, graphed according to seasonal appearances, and containing many specifics of site locations. They are very handy in the field. You should obtain one for the areas you frequent in order to determine what birds are expected there and when. Local museums or Audubon societies usually publish these. Rickert's volume on bird clubs also includes information on checklists, local publications and booklets.

RECORDS AND TAPES

Records are available to help you get started learning bird calls and songs. However, they are no substitute for actual hours spent in the field. The best way to learn bird sounds is by carefully tracking down a call until you locate the bird. More experienced birders can help greatly in this process. Then, the records and tapes can be used at home to reinforce your familiarity with the birds you heard on your field trip.

If you have the proper equipment, you can make your own tapes from published records and tapes. You can record any combination of bird songs you choose, and create special tapes for special bird trips, in order to learn the sounds of new birds you will encounter.

The Laboratory of Ornithology at Cornell University is noted for its bird recordings. They offer an extensive catalog of selections. We have listed it (and other catalogs) in the Appendix. For beginners, the records coordinated with the Eastern and Western Peterson guides are the best. Of course, there are numerous other fine recordings of bird sounds. Another possibility is a battery powered microphonograph that plays prerecorded discs of bird songs. This equipment is very portable and easy to use; it is called *The Audible Audubon*.

When listening to bird records, keep in mind it is easier to transcribe songs than calls. After reading Chapter Three, you will learn that birds make a variety of noises, other than their spring songs. These other calls are probably best learned in the field. If you combine listening to records with hours spent outdoors birdwatching, your memory of bird sounds will dramatically improve.

3. What to Look For?

So...you've decided to go out and start looking at birds. But, what do you look for when you first spot an unfamiliar bird? Beginning birdwatchers are always anxious to know "How to tell one bird from another," as if there were some secret formula that, once learned, would make bird identification a snap.

Identifying birds resembles solving a puzzle; this is the intrigue of birding. Many small, simple pieces of information are fitted together before you arrive at a recognition of the whole bird. Special clues will point you in the direction of the correct species. This chapter will concentrate on the major characteristics of the bird in front of you, and will teach you which specifics to carefully observe. The more practice you have, the more quickly you will come to the right answer.

You may worry if you only have a brief moment to focus your binoculars before the bird has flown. This element of birding makes the puzzle a little more difficult. Birds tend to fly away unexpectedly—and often very fast! Unlike the study of wildflowers, butterflies, shells or mammals, birding means a glimpse here, a flash of wing bars there, and sometimes total frustration to the observer.

Be patient, go slowly, and begin with the common birds you see around your backyard, a nearby park or on the way to work. Choose a familiar environment. Give yourself time to get your binoculars up, focus and notice the key points we will teach you in this chapter. You will see that bird again! And, each time you see it you will absorb a bit more until you can form a mental image of that species. Finally, you will be able to recognize the bird anywhere.

The bird species you will see have all evolved over eons and now live more or less specialized lives. Specialization can be seen in their bodies and their behaviors in ways you can clearly spot. If you know something about how a bird's body functions, you will know a lot about how it lives. To give a silly illustration: you won't find an eagle at your hummingbird feeder. Eagles and hummingbirds live in very different ways. They eat different kinds of food, fly differently and their bodies are shaped differently. You can easily see the differences between the two birds, and you will use these clues in your process of identification.

This chapter will teach you the basic steps to use in solving the puzzles of bird identification. We have broken it down into the following five sections. SILHOUETTE will discuss the first thing you should notice about a bird: its shape and relative size. PLUMAGE follows and shows you how to distinguish the patterns of color and feather arrangements which form the key field marks. Another crucial part to the puzzle is the BEHAVIOR of the bird, how it is flying, searching for food or whatever. The HABITAT where you found the bird—forest, seashore, grassland, or any other environment—can give you a great deal of information. With habitat, we also consider the bird's distribution or geographic range. And lastly, the bird's own VOICE will help your diagnosis.

Use these clues systematically on your birding trips. Your accuracy will improve quickly, and so will your understanding of the birds. With time you will find you need to recognize only one or two features of the bird to make an accurate field identification.

SILHOUETTE

Let's study the most important clue to bird identification first. By silhouette we mean the relative size and shape of the bird. Most beginners assume you notice the bird's color first when you look through your binoculars. However, strange as it may seem, color is often not as important as the overall size and shape of the bird. In Chapter Four we have described and illustrated the general silhouettes of the bird families. These will form the basis of your identification.

Don't worry about color, voice or such markings as wing bars and head stripes until you have a good idea of which family the bird belongs to. Is it a vireo, warbler, finch, or starling? Once you know the family, you can figure out the individual species more easily. Bird guides emphasizing identification by color are not very successful because they ignore silhouette. For instance, a "medium-sized brown bird" could be anything from a thrush to a towhee to a plover to a cowbird. However, each one of these birds has a characteristic shape that would have told you its family even if you never saw the color of the bird.

Some generalizations about silhouettes of birds are easy to make. Birds with long legs are waders and spend their time in watery environments where long, slender legs are a definite advantage. Predators have sharp beaks and hooked claws for grabbing and killing their prey. Birds with a large wingspan are capable of extended periods of time in the air, maneuvering easily with the wind. The more you study birds, the more you will see how their bodies are shaped for the lives they live.

Study the bird's size first. Field guides give the tip-to-tail measurements of every bird, but you may find this information isn't helpful when you are in the field spotting an unfamiliar species. You need an informal scale in your mind to judge relative bird sizes. We emphasize relativity here because such adjectives as "large" or "tiny" become meaningless if they are not tied to a few birds you already know. Ask yourself, "Is that tiny bird even smaller than a House Sparrow?" Try to visualize the relative sizes of some birds you see every day. You might think of "small" birds as being six inches or under, like the House Sparrow. A "medium" bird might be around ten inches, like the American Robin, or up to twelve inches, like the common pigeon. Crows could be thought of as "large" birds at about seventeen inches. Any bird larger than a crow could be classified as "very large," including most of the buteo hawks, geese and Great Blue Herons.

Many field guides, particularly those illustrated by artists, will tend to confuse you with drawings that vary in scale from page to page. Tiny flycatchers may be pictured as large as thrushes to illustrate minute characteristics used in distinguishing each group. Remember, consult the measurements given in the text and then compare them with your knowledge of common backyard bird sizes.

Another pitfall for beginners is the size of birds when viewed through binoculars. In the field it takes practice to allow for the distortion that occurs as you scan with binoculars. Birdwatchers rely on this enlargement to observe key field marks at a distance. At the start, you may find yourself wondering why such a small bird as a wood-pewee can look fairly large through the binoculars. This is another reason to develop your own scale of size relative to the birds you already know. With experience you will automatically compensate for the size distortion you see through your binoculars.

The more birds you recognize on sight, the more you can judge relative sizes. For instance, you are scanning a group of shorebirds you know to be Willets. They are standing on a nearby mudflat with heads tucked under their wings. One bird is conspicuously larger, however. You might guess it is a Whimbrel or a Marbled Godwit, both common shorebirds larger than a Willet. At last the bird raises its head to reveal a long, pinkish bill with a slight uptilt at the tip. Since the Whimbrel has a bill that curves downward, you conclude this might be a Marbled Godwit. The size of the bird was the first clue you used in identification, the shape of the bill was the second.

After size, the most important part of the bird's silhouette is the shape of the bill, because bill shapes form major clues to bird families. Is the bill long or short, thick or thin? Does it curve up or down? Is it hooked at the tip? If you have time to see only one part of the bird focus on the head and the shape of the bill.

Specific bill shapes distinguish one family of birds from another, so you should notice this aspect of the silhouette carefully. Finches, such as the House Finch, American Goldfinch and Common Redpoll have small conical bills efficient at cracking open seeds. Flycatchers show slender bills with fine hairs at the base that enable them to snare insects on the wing. The kingfisher's bill is dagger-like and strong to handle the fish it devours. Warblers have needle-like bills for gleaning insects from leaves. These variations in bill size and shape often restrict a species to certain foods. These minute details of specialization permit them to fit into similar habitats without one endangering the survival of others. We may not be sure exactly which seeds, insects or fruits will be eaten by which bird in our backyard, but generally we can use the shape of their bills to help us identify their families.

Kites, hawks, eagles and falcons possess sharp, hooked beaks suitable for ripping and tearing live flesh. Sighting one of these birds in your binoculars you should immediately recognize it as a predator. From a distance, the Northern Mockingbird and the Loggerhead Shrike might appear alike due to their gray and white coloration. But take a look at their heads. The shrike's fierce, thick beak with the hooked tip is used for impaling prey on thorns or barbed wire fences. The thinner bill of the mockingbird reflects its lifestyle and shows it as an omnivore.

It would be convenient if we could simply say a bird's eating habits were always reflected in a certain bill shape. However, in some cases you will be forced to memorize a particular bill shape just because it represents a specific bird family. For example, the vireo bill is somewhat thicker than that of a wood warbler, yet they both feed largely on the same grubs and insects. In this instance, form a "vireo image" in your mind so you can recognize it and its bill shape in the future.

Dunlin

Whimbrel

Black Turnstone

With shorebirds, the shape of the bill will lead you not only to the family, but also to the exact species. For example, Long-billed Curlews and Whimbrels have decurved bills, each of a different length. Dowitchers have very long bills in proportion to their chunky bodies. Turnstones possess small, pigeon-like bills. The Dunlin's bill is sturdy with a slight droop at the end. All these birds are in the sandpiper family.

Tail shapes are further components of the bird's silhouette for you to check. Does the bird have a blunt, tailless look like a starling? Does it have a tapered, pointed tail like a Mourning Dove? You can distinguish the accipiter hawks from the buteo hawks in flight by the tail shape. The former's is thin while the buteo's are broad. Within the accipiter genus, you can tell the difference between a Sharp-shinned Hawk with its squared-off tail from a Cooper's Hawk with its rounded tail. Ravens and crows are both large, dark birds, but in flight the raven's tail is wedge-shaped and the crow's is fan-shaped. Most North American swallows look similar in flight; however, the Barn Swallow is easily spotted by its deeply forked tail. Terns, too, have a forked tail which helps distinguish them from the gulls.

Wing shapes are helpful when you see the bird's silhouette in flight overhead. Swifts have thin, bowed wings that arch backward; swallows appear similar but they have wider wings with the bend of the wrist further out. Terns have pointed wings sharply bent at the elbow; gulls do not. The rounded wings of the accipiters, like the Sharp-shinned Hawk, differ from the pointed wings of the falcons, like the American Kestrel. With these clues to a bird's flight silhouette, you can identify species from a great distance.

Western Gull

Forster's Tern

To sum up, when looking at the silhouette of a bird observe its relative size and overall body shape first. Then study the head for the bill shape which will give you a clue to the bird's family. Finally, if you have a chance, check the wing and tail shapes in flight.

PLUMAGE

Next, study the bird's plumage. As we pointed out in the section on silhouettes, most beginning birdwatchers tend to notice this feature first. Look at the color and pattern of the bird's feathers. Birdwatchers call the key identifying portions of the bird's plumage the "field marks." Some examples are wing bars (or lack of them), white in the tail corners, a spotted breast, eye ring, etc. All these bits of information are extremely helpful to the birder.

In recognizing the field marks it is useful to learn the parts of a typical bird. Field guides will describe birds using terms such as "primaries," "scapulars" and "undertail coverts." To make a positive identification of some confusing species you will have to know which feathers they are referring to. Also, when describing a bird in your notes or to another bird-watcher, you will want to communicate accurately the bird's appearance. The following illustration shows the names of the most frequently described parts of a typical bird.

Begin with the bird's head, again. Important field marks are often concentrated in the head pattern. For instance, what color is the line through the eye, does it have an eyebrow (supercilium), is there an eye ring? Does the bird have striping on the crown? How about the chin, the throat, the nape—what color are they? Is the feathering between the eye and the bill (the lore) pale? Does it connect with the eye ring to form a "spectacled" look?

Here are some examples of how diagnostic head markings can help you identify birds. The adult Golden-crowned Sparrow is told from the adult White-crowned Sparrow by the yellow patch that separates its two black crown stripes. The White-crowned, on the other hand, has a bold black and white striped head pattern. The Swainson's and Gray-cheeked Thrushes appear similar until you notice the Swainson's has buffy lores and a bold buffy eye ring. The Gray-cheeked has only an indistinct eye ring and no buffy lores. With a glance at the head markings, you can tell the two species of kinglets apart. The male Golden-crowned Kinglet has an orange crown patch bordered in yellow and black. The male Ruby-crowned Kinglet usually shows no head patch at all, except when it

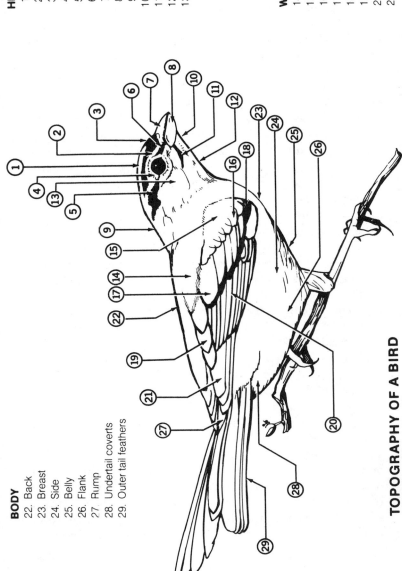

TOPOGRAPHY OF A BIRD

HEAD
1. Crown
2. Eyebrow (supercilium)
3. Forehead
4. Eye ring
5. Eye line
6. Lore
7. Upper mandible
8. Lower mandible
9. Nape
10. Chin
11. Whisker (malar line)
12. Throat
13. Ear patch (auricular)

WINGS
14. Scapulars
15. Lesser wing coverts
16. Median wing coverts
17. Greater wing coverts
18. Wing bar
19. Tertials
20. Secondaries
21. Primaries

BODY
22. Back
23. Breast
24. Side
25. Belly
26. Flank
27. Rump
28. Undertail coverts
29. Outer tail feathers

becomes agitated and erects the crimson feathers on its crown.

After observing the head, look at the rest of the bird for any prominent field marks. For instance, in identifying male hummingbirds the color of the brilliant throat patch (gorget) is important. The color of the wing tips (primaries) on adult and juvenile gulls can be crucial. Many field marks are best seen when the bird is in flight. Dark shoulder (patagial) marks help distinguish a Red-tailed Hawk from below. When flying, the Northern Flicker has a prominent white rump.

Many ducks will show key field marks through a scope that can tell you their species instantly. The white crescent on the head and the corresponding crescent on the flank indicate a male Blue-winged Teal. The male Surf Scoter has a white patch on his forehead, nape and bill. A fan-shaped white head patch will identify the male Hooded Merganser, when its crest is raised. Once again, we are looking at the head for important clues.

Some birds you will learn to distinguish by color alone because they are so brilliantly visible. Among this group are the Red-winged Blackbird, Northern Cardinal, Vermilion Flycatcher, and the Eastern and Western Bluebirds. Remember, though, the females are not as brightly colored as the males.

Consult a field guide to learn field marks and male/female plumage variations. Most field guides are incredibly successful at portraying bird plumages whether they use photographs or paintings.

So far, we have been talking about adult plumages. However, plumages vary depending upon the season, the bird's age and its sex. You may be surprised when looking through a field guide to discover that some birds look very different in their breeding plumages than in their winter plumages. Also you may be struck by plumage differences between the males and females of the same species. When reading about plumage variations it can sound so bewildering you will wonder how to recognize anything. However, knowing the silhouettes really helps. Many birdwatchers confine their identifications to adult birds. You will probably want to as well, until you have more experience in the field.

We will give you a brief overview of changes of plumage, or

molt, so you can have some idea of the complexities involved. Molt refers to the periodic replacement of feathers. All adult birds molt at least once a year, sometimes even two or three times. In Chapter One we pointed out how important feathers are to the life of birds. These appendages are so essential that birds replace them often to maintain their efficiency. Too, birds need different kinds of feathers at different times of their lives. A newly-hatched nestling has different requirements from a full-sized adult, and a male seeking nesting territory and a mate in the spring needs to advertise his presence much more than he does in the winter.

When birds are in the nest they wear a soft, fluffy cover of *down*. Their first coat of true feathers is called the *juvenile* plumage. They may molt one or more times before they assume the *adult* plumage. These molts are variously called *immature* or *subadult* plumages. Once the bird reaches adulthood, it may assume a *winter* plumage (sometimes called *basic* plumage), and in many species it is followed by a more colorful *breeding* (sometimes called *alternate*) plumage.

Each species follows its own pattern of molts, and they vary considerably. The plumages we have named above do not all occur in every bird. For instance, some species do not have discrete immature plumages. Cormorants and pelicans molt almost continuously through their first year or two. Many birds wear more brilliantly colorful plumage in the spring and summer than in the fall and winter.

Many birds come into their winter or nonbreeding plumage during late summer and early fall. For instance, almost all shorebirds assume a somber gray-and-white winter plumage around this time, in contrast to the rich tones of their breeding attire. Male grosbeaks and buntings also show a more subdued coloration when they molt into fall or winter plumage. Many water birds, such as loons, grebes, geese and swans, lose all their flight feathers then, rendering them virtually flightless. Male ducks, after the breeding season, assume a dull basic plumage (often called *eclipse*) that closely resembles the female's.

In the spring many birds go through a partial molt, intensifying the color of the male's plumage and making it brighter than the female's. For example, male American and Lesser Goldfinches appear in brighter yellow and black plumage after their spring molt. Still other species achieve a more brilliant breeding plumage without going through a molt. The male House Sparrow and Bobolink acquire their spring attire through the gradual wearing away of the tips of their feathers. In the European Starling, the white tips of the feathers wear away so their speckled look of the fall is transformed to glossy black by spring.

Remember, not all species of birds show seasonal plumage changes and not all species show differences between the males and females. Sometimes both the males and females will change with the season, sometimes only the males do, and sometimes neither sex changes appearance. The male Scarlet Tanager has a crimson coat during the breeding season only. At other seasons it is yellow-green like the female. The male and female Anna's Hummingbirds always appear different, no matter what the season. Male and female Spotted Sandpipers both assume a breeding plumage, but it is exactly alike. On the other hand, male and female House Wrens and Northern Mockingbirds are examples of species that look alike year-round, regardless of the season.

After young birds have hatched and molted into their juvenile plumages, you may observe family groups with individuals showing a distinctly different plumage from the parent birds. Smaller perching birds retain their juvenile plumage for only one or two months in the summer. They are usually found in the same flock with the adults, or at least nearby, which helps in recognizing them. Larger birds, such as eagles and gulls, take two or three years to reach maturity. In studying gulls especially, it is necessary to know there are several sub-adult plumages. However, beginning birders may wish to postpone mastering other gull plumages until they are thoroughly familiar with the adults'.

As you can readily see, a discussion of plumage variations quickly gets complicated. This is one reason we emphasize learning the basic silhouettes first. They can provide an instant clue to identification no matter what plumage the bird is wearing. If you have a good field guide for your area, the major plumage variations should be illustrated. You will learn them as you pick up more and more details about the birds that interest you.

Briefly, when you are starting to look at plumage differences as a means of identification, train your eye to spot key field marks first, especially in the head area. Then try to pick up any other prominent field marks or color patterns. Use these, along with your knowledge of silhouette, to zero in on the correct species. At first, pay most attention to adult birds; with experience you can begin to spot the immatures or those in less typical plumages.

BEHAVIOR

Beginners may find it hard to believe, but some birds can be identified by their behavior alone. Ask yourself this question: "What was the bird doing when I saw it?" It was probably either searching for food or flying away, right? Birds have mannerisms characteristic of their families and sometimes they are characteristic of particular species within those families.

Let's consider some feeding behaviors to begin. If the bird you see is just sitting there, notice its posture. Flycatchers, for instance, sit up straight with their tails hanging down. They often flick or wag their tails repeatedly. In hunting for food, they have a special way of flying out from their perch, nabbing an insect, and returning to the same spot or another prominent twig. All flycatchers do this, and birders have named it "flycatching behavior" because it is so unique. Other birds, like warblers, may adopt flycatching behavior temporarily but they never sit erect and they never repeat this behavior time after time.

Nuthatches search the bark of trees for food by travelling down headfirst. On the other hand, creepers and woodpeckers spiral up the tree trunks. Goldfinches cling to weed and thistle tops in fields, extracting the seeds. Notice how sluggish the vireos are in searching the treetops for food when compared to the warblers, who tumble and flutter rapidly in the branches.

You will find the shorebird families use assorted methods for finding little worms, snails and crustaceans in the mudflats. Sanderlings scurry up and down the open beach following the foamy edges of the waves as they wash up and back. Dowitchers exhibit a "sewing machine" movement as they rapidly poke their bills up and down, seeming to stitch in the shallow tidal pools. Plovers search for food by running a little way, then pausing, then running on. Greater and Lesser Yellowlegs walk rapidly through shallow water, changing direction frequently from side to side and making little dashes here and there to scare up insects. In deeper pools Wilson's Phalaropes whirl around and around like tops on the surface of the water, then they jab with their bills at all the tiny creatures they have stirred up. American Avocets walk rapidly through the water, sweeping their long, recurved bills from side to side.

Wandering Tattler

Interestingly, many behavior characteristics of birds are tied to special tail movements and postures. All wrens hold their tails cocked up from their body. The Hermit Thrush slowly raises and lowers its tail when pausing on the forest floor to explore for food. It also nervously flicks its wings from time to time. The Spotted Sandpiper and the Wandering Tattler bob their rear ends constantly when walking. The Blue-gray Gnatcatcher and the Sage Sparrow jerk their tails in an upright position. Flycatchers in the *Empidonax* genus can be identified by whether they first bob their tails up or down when perched. Don't laugh, this is an important clue! The Gray Flycatcher's tail goes down then up, other *Empidonaxes* flop their tails up then down.

Watch how birds behave in exposed places and on the ground. Dippers and Rock Wrens have a habit of doing "deep knee bends" on exposed rocks. Sparrows hop on the ground whereas Pipits and Horned Larks walk on the ground. Towhees and Fox Sparrows scratch vigorously in dry leaves, feet together, forward and backward to disturb little grubs. Pigeons and blackbirds, coots and pipits pump their heads forward as they move about. Being aware of these little behavioral quirks can eliminate many similar species, even if you can't fully see the bird's plumage pattern or color.

Let's look at flight behavior, too. You may already be familiar with the deeply undulating flight of the members of the woodpecker family. Other birds fly straight with rapidly beating wings like pigeons and doves, while some seem to have a weak flight from bush to treetop, like bushtits and titmice. At the shore, practice telling the difference between loons and cormorants in flight. Loons have a peculiar "bowed" look with head and tail seemingly held lower than the rapidly beating wings. Cormorants have the same rapid wing beat, but hold their bodies level or tilted slightly upward and forward in flight.

Some birds of prey hover in a stationary position when hunting, like the American Kestrel, and the Ferruginous and Roughlegged Hawks. Others, like the Northern Harrier, fly low over open country, rocking from side to side. A Turkey Vulture also has this tilting flight pattern, although it usually stays high in the sky. Golden Eagles and Condors soar with their huge wings spread perfectly horizontal and steady.

Many other types of behavior distinguish bird species, too. Field guides and bird books often use descriptive adjectives to give you clues to typical bird behaviors. Rails are often called secretive, whereas jays are considered aggressive. These obvious, but often difficult to define, qualities can help a great deal in field identification. As a beginner you should concentrate on feeding and flight behavior. Study the common birds in your backyard year-round to learn other distinguishing behaviors. Soon you will be able to put together a picture of how bird behavior can be used to identify a species.

American Black Oystercatcher

HABITAT

We've talked about silhouette, plumage and behavior as important ways of distinguishing between birds. What about the bird's habitat requirements? Birds are specialized and have preferences for where they live. Of course, habitat needs differ and some birds may be able to live over much of North America whereas others can exist in only very restricted localities.

Most birds have a fairly well-defined geographical range in which they normally occur at different times of the year. Usually each species occupies a breeding range to nest and raise young, then moves to a wintering range for the rest of the year. A bird's distribution delineates where you can find the bird at specific times of the year. It is helpful to know the distribution of a species in any given location because the seasons of the year can bring changes in a particular bird's abundance. When you venture out birding in the winter months in your area you will see winter residents and these often will be different from the summer residents. Of course, some birds will be permanent residents, that is, they remain year-round. Local checklists of your region provide this information.

Within its general range, each species lives by preference in a certain habitat. A knowledge of habitat is essential if you are going to seek out any specific bird. For example, you tend not to find shorebirds feeding on the dry desert floor. Grassland birds will not inhabit mudflats, and waders won't be found in swift-running mountain streams.

Habitat is the set of specific environmental conditions that must be met for the survival of the bird. These may include weather, types of vegetation, altitude, proximity to water, soil type, sunlight, presence of appropriate food and safe nesting spots. We don't know all the habitat needs of the birds we view. Many may be too subtle to interpret without a lifetime of study. Each habitat has its characteristic communities of animal and plant life, and we should be aware of this when we are birdwatching. If you take field trips to assorted habitats you can expect to see a wide variety of bird species.

The following is a rough listing of habitats you can find in the continental United States. Remember these are broad categories and within any particular one you will find diversification depending upon such factors as altitude and amount of rainfall.

HABITATS
Tundra
Coniferous Forests
Deciduous Forests
Grasslands
Deserts
Freshwater Lakes, Ponds and Streams
Shores and Marshes
Seas

The listing below is a more detailed example of bird habitats that might occur near the central California coast.

COASTAL AQUATIC HABITATS
Open Ocean
Inshore Waters, Harbors, Rocky, and Sandy Beaches
Marshes and Estuaries

LOWLANDS
Stream and Canyon Woodland
Oak Woodland and Savanna
Chaparral
Agricultural, Residential and Urban Developments
Freshwater Marshes, Rivers, Lakes and Reservoirs

MOUNTAINS
Coniferous Forest
Rocky Habitats and Montane Chaparral
Pinon-juniper, Semi-desert Scrub, Sage
High Plains

Using the above districts for reference, let us say you find yourself on the shores of a large freshwater lake, and you spot a couple of cormorants sitting on a dead log by the water's edge. Three species of cormorants are common on the west coast, but you know that the Double-crested is the only one found on inland bodies of water, as well as on rocky seashores. Brandt's and Pelagic Cormorants almost never wander inland. By knowing the bird's distribution, you narrowed it down to the three possible species of cormorant, and by knowing habitat preferences, you have a good clue that the birds on the log are Double-crested Cormorants.

The House Sparrow (sometimes called the English Sparrow) is an example of a bird which has completely adapted to man's urban environment, now its preferred habitat. Introduced to this country in the 1850s, House Sparrows have thrived at cafe tables and park benches, flocking to feed on garbage in street gutters and sidewalks. They are prepared to build their bulky nests in eaves and roof tiles, or the nooks and crannies of city buildings. The House Sparrow's aggressive behavior has even succeeded in supplanting other birds who can't compete as well near human habitation.

Within the same habitat, birds manage to survive in diverse ways, enabling them all to make a living in the same small area. In other words, they occupy separate niches. Within a given habitat you will see certain birds foraging for food from characteristic locations. The following examples aren't hard and fast rules, but they will show you how some common birds sort themselves out to obtain the food they require.

Towhees will scratch amongst the dead leaves on the forest floor to disturb grubs and seeds on ground level. Other types of sparrows inhabit more open, weedy fields. Wood-pewees prefer the middle levels about twenty feet off the ground, sallying forth from exposed branches to capture passing insects. Nuthatches, creepers and woodpeckers work tree trunks scavenging for morsels hidden in the bark. Warblers and vireos are usually found high in the canopy where they explore the undersides of leaves, flitting from branch to branch in their hurried search. Nearby phone poles or the tops of tall trees are good perches for kestrels, where they scan the surrounding area for grasshoppers and rodents. High overhead, Red-tailed Hawks soar lazily, hunting for prey. Way, way up, the swifts take their food on the wing, seldom perching at all.

Obviously these examples won't always hold true, particularly when birds are migrating. But you are not likely to see a towhee atop a tall pine tree. Nor are you apt to see an Olive-sided Flycatcher perched a foot off the ground. Knowing a bird's general range distribution, and habitat preference within that range, can help you enormously in identifying it.

VOICE

We mention this aspect of identification last, but by the time you have been birding awhile it could be the first and only clue you need to correctly tell the species of bird in question. Part of birdwatching is the heightened awareness that allows you to notice small details. While you are expanding your power of observation, be sure to really listen to the sounds of the bird in front of you. If you hear an unknown call, search the trees and undergrowth until you can locate the bird. In a surprisingly short time, your memory will retain the call and you will recognize it, and the bird, on subsequent trips.

Birds have a number of vocalizations. Songs are a complex series of sounds usually used in the spring to attract mates and to proclaim breeding territories. Calls are simpler than songs and can be employed for many different purposes including to indicate aggression or alarm, to broadcast an individual's location, etc. We use the term "calls" to refer to any sound a bird utters that is not a full song. "Chips," for example, are the short, staccato notes often given by warblers and sparrows. Thus, chips are a kind of call. Another bird sound, given in flight, is designated a flight call. For example, an Orange-crowned Warbler possesses a spring song, a metallic chip and a *"seep"* flight call. A Northern Mockingbird, on the other hand, sings a number of songs and utters several characteristic calls, but it does not chip.

It takes time to learn which song or chip comes from which bird. Listening to the birds outside your window can be a rewarding way to begin. Practice recognizing the raspy scolding quality of a wren's voice, the nagging squawk of a jay, the delicate song of a warbler in spring, the flute-like whistle of an oriole's song, the phrased warble of a vireo or the squeak of a woodpecker. Each species has its own unique calls and songs. However, certain bird families exhibit generalized qualities in their sounds. Start by listening to these. Then, when you hear a warbler chip it will alert you to the presence of a warbler nearby, even if you are not sure which kind of warbler it is. Just as in learning the silhouettes of birds, you can distinguish resemblances in bird calls and songs by families.

It is somewhat like deciphering a new and secret language. Constant exposure and a desire to try are all you need. Listening to records and tapes helps, but not as much as getting outside and finding the birds yourself. Birdwatching with a more knowledgeable birder can be a real advantage in learning bird calls. Ask your field trip leader or class teacher to identify all the different calls around you. If they know, they will be glad to share it with you. You may be surprised, however, at how many so-called experts don't know bird calls as they should.

In any given forest or riparian area you can only locate about half of the bird population by sight alone. If you learn to recognize bird sounds, however, you will increase your bird counts considerably. Bird calls can alert you to a bird's presence in hard-to-view leafy and brushy habitats. Skilled birders strolling through a woodland need to lift their binoculars less frequently, as they are able to identify birds by calls alone. You can learn these sounds, too. Practice in a familiar place, and ask questions of the experts. Bird calls will become intelligible to you over time, just as any new language.

We have outlined the five major clues to bird identification: SILHOUETTE, PLUMAGE, BEHAVIOR, HABITAT, and VOICE. At any one time you will probably need only two or, at most, three of these bits of information to know a bird. After many hours of field trips and poking around your neighborhood, you will find yourself seeing a bird and automatically recognizing it without consciously going through all of the steps we have listed. You will gather an impression of the bird's overall form and its behavior, and these will add up to its essential character in the field. You will automatically know the bird, whether it is a Rufous-sided Towhee, an Ovenbird or a Willet. Birders call this birding by "gestalt," or, as the British say, recognizing the "jizz" of the bird. As a bird flashes across the path or scuttles under a garden shrub, you can call out "Song Sparrow" or "House Wren" without stopping to consciously analyze every feature of the bird. Of course, you certainly would not identify a rarity this way, but with common birds you can reach this level of birdwatching rather quickly. And that is when it really starts to be fun!

4. The Bird Families

HOW TO USE THIS CHAPTER

What is a buteo, a finch, a sparrow? It doesn't help much on your first bird walk when the leader identifies a towhee as "another sparrow." How are birds classified, and what common characteristics can you find in each classification?

Despite what scientists say about similarities and dissimilarities in skeleton or egg-white protein, you still have to know in the field what an unfamiliar bird is and why it is classified with an altogether different bird. This chapter will show you the outstanding characteristics of the families of birds sighted in North America. You will feel much more comfortable on your birding trips when you can tell the general categories of birds you sight, and when you know a bit about what they feed on, where they live, and what functions their various body types fulfill.

While you read this chapter, study the silhouettes and try to remember the outstanding characteristics of each family. Also, study the pictures in a good field guide. Or, better still, stroll through the bird room of the nearest natural history museum. Look at specimens and learn their relative sizes and characteristic plumages. This will give you a solid background for your field work. A familiarity with the bird families is the first step in identification, and will vastly improve your accuracy in the field.

THE BIRD FAMILIES

Scientists arrange plants and animals in increasingly narrow categories, from the kingdom at the top all the way down to each individual species at the bottom. The number of individuals in each group decreases as the similarity between them increases, until you arrive at the particular species you wish to describe. The names are in Latin, so scientists all over the world will know which species they are discussing, although a number of common names may exist in other languages. For example, let's look at the classification of the Arctic Tern, and how it gets its Latin name, *Sterna paradisaea*.

Kingdom:	*Animalia* (animals)
Phylum:	*Chordata* (animals with notochord)
Subphyllum:	*Vertebrata* (animals with backbone)
Class:	*Aves* (birds)
Order:	*Charadriiformes* (includes such birds as gulls, terns, auks, plovers)
Family:	*Laridae* (includes only gulls & terns)
Genus:	*Sterna* (includes only closely related terns)
Species:	*paradisaea* (the Arctic Tern)

Each bird has a scientific Latin name in two parts, the genus and the species. Genus names, *Sterna* in this case, are capitalized, while species names, *paradisaea* here, are not.

There is one further classification you should understand: subspecies. In field guides you will run across this term or its synonym, race. Subspecies are populations of birds within a given species that show distinct plumage differences when compared to others in that species. These variations are usually by geographic region, and it may take some practice to spot the differences between subspecies in the field. However, these birds are capable of interbreeding and therefore are not considered to be separate species. A third Latin name is added to designate subspecies. For example, *Passerella iliaca stephensi* is a Fox Sparrow that resides in southern California in the summer. Whereas, *Passerella iliaca altavagans* is a Fox Sparrow that breeds on the east side of the Rockies in western Canada. As a beginner, you should understand the concept of subspecies, but you will probably not be concerned with identifying them.

As you can see from the example of the Arctic Tern above, the class *Aves* (birds) is divided into orders, and the orders are further grouped into families. For a beginner, the families are the most important. In most cases, there exists sufficient similarity between the birds within each family for you to learn their general characteristics. Learning the families is the first step in learning bird identification, and it is covered in this chapter.

The arrangement of "order, family, genus, species" is based on the presumed evolutionary development of each group of birds. The most primitive order—the loons—is listed first, while the most advanced—the perching birds or *Passeriformes*—comes last. These categories are defined after decades of scientific study, and are standardized by the American Ornithologists' Union. Birds are not switched from family to family, or from subspecies to species, without substantial basis. From time to time, the A.O.U. makes changes in this taxonomic organization. These changes may result in certain species of birds being lumped into one category, or occasionally a species is split into several new ones. These changes are based on scientific knowledge and are not made lightly.

Checklists are always organized according to the most recent taxonomic order, field guides usually are. When reading these you may find confusing discrepancies in names, based on when the book was published. Fortunately, these changes do not occur frequently and are easily learned, once you understand the basic principles involved.

Unlike Latin names, common names have been assigned haphazardly and often for reasons that no longer seem apparent. It is confusing to find birds with different common names in the same scientific categories, and the American Ornithologists' Union is now standardizing common names of North American birds. In the descriptions below and throughout the book you will find common names under family designations so you can easily see, for instance, that egrets and bitterns are all in the heron (*Ardeidae*) family. Some bird families have only one representative species in this country, others have many. If you think of the bird world as a structured whole, organized by orders, families, genuses, species and subspecies you will find field identification much easier.

LOONS *(Gaviidae)*

Common Loon

These are swimming birds with webbed feet; toes are four in number, the front three connected by webs. They are fairly large, bigger than ducks, with dagger-like bills. Their legs are set far back on their bodies, a disadvantage for maneuvering on land, but of great help in their underwater pursuit of fish. Loons spend 95% of their time on the water, except when incubating eggs. They are exceptionally good divers, and feed on fish and other marine animals. In flight, they present a hunchbacked shape with a drooping neck. They breed in freshwater lakes and winter along the coasts.

GREBES *(Podicipedidae)*

Red-necked Grebe

This is another group of swimming birds, with shorter bodies than the loons, and lobed feet. Lobes are flaps along their toes that enable them to swim quite well. Like the loons, they paddle with both feet at once. They sit low in the water with a tailless look. By altering their specific gravity, they can lower themselves in the water until only the head or bill shows. They have thin necks and pointed bills (except the Pied-billed). They feed on marine animals, crustaceans and aquatic insects by diving. Grebes are generally smaller than loons, their legs are set far back on their bodies.

ALBATROSSES *(Diomedeidae)*

These are large birds with long, narrow,

tapering wings that give them outstanding flight capacity. Their wingspread is about six or seven feet in species sighted near the United States. They spend most of their time on the oceans feeding on surface fish or squid, and sometimes scavenging garbage from ships. Albatrosses have amazing endurance; they are capable of long sustained flight for days over the ocean, alighting only on the surface to feed. These birds are tubenoses, with long tube-shaped nostrils on their bills. Like many other birds (such as cormorants, boobies, gulls, grebes, etc.) albatrosses have salt glands in their skulls to excrete body fluids, without using the kidneys. In the tubenoses, the ducts of these glands convey the concentrated salt solution to the nostrils, where it trickles out through the unique tube-like covering. This process eliminates their need for fresh water. All tubenoses, which include the next two families, have webbed feet. Albatrosses are only rarely seen from shore, usually they are viewed at sea.

SHEARWATERS, PETRELS and FULMARS *(Procellariidae)*

This family is a group of seabirds approximately gull-sized, but with narrower wings. They live on the open seas and occasionally are seen from the shore. They breed in colonies on oceanic islands, nesting in shallow burrows. They feed by diving after fish and crustaceans from the ocean's surface, often using their wings for underwater pursuit. They are tubenosed. You can learn to identify their flight, which consists of several flaps alter-

Sooty Shearwater

nating with stiff-winged glides as they skim low over the waves.

STORM-PETRELS *(Hydrobatidae)*

These small seabirds also have tubenoses to help remove excess salt from their bodies. A distinctive feature of the birds of this order is a peculiar stomach oil which can be ejected when the bird is disturbed. This has a strong, musky odor that pervades the bird and its breeding area. They fly close to the ocean surface with their wings bent at the "wrist" and wave-hop to pluck fish or refuse from the surface. The individual species are usually identified by size and rump pattern as well as by flight pattern. They are seen only on pelagic trips.

TROPICBIRDS *(Phaethontidae)*

These medium-sized marine birds are boldly marked in black and white. The adults possess greatly elongated central tail feathers. Unlike gulls, they fly with quick wingbeats. They are birds of the tropics and occasionally visit the United States. The White-tailed and Red-billed Tropicbird are rare but regular visitors in the Gulf of Mexico and off the California coast.

GANNETS and BOOBIES *(Sulidae)*

Northern Gannet

A group of large seabirds with webbed feet, most gannets and boobies are black and white. All have long pointed bills, pointed tails, and tapered wings. They capture fish with high, sudden dives from the air. They are colonial nesters on sea islands. Gannets are common off the East Coast; boobies are rare visitors everywhere but in the Gulf of Mexico.

PELICANS *(Pelecanidae)*

This is a group of very large waterbirds with paddlefeet where all four toes are joined by webbing, as contrasted with three toes for the ducks. There are only two species found in the United States. Pelicans have enormous bills with large pouches underneath for scooping up fish. They fly with their head held back on their shoulders, often in orderly diagonal lines, with each bird flapping then gliding in rhythm. The Brown Pelican plunges into the water from flight to obtain fish. Air sacs under their skin cushion the impact and help bring them up again always facing the wind, ready to take off. They nest in colonies. The Brown Pelican was endangered in parts of its range by DDT in its food chain, before this pesticide was banned.

Brown Pelican

CORMORANTS *(Phalacrocoracidae)*

These large water birds have webbed feet and slim, long bills with a strong hook at the tip. Cormorants are usually blackish, with snake-like thin necks. They hold their slender bill tilted upward. When floating on the water, they have a partially submerged look. They are powerful fliers and are found on rocky coasts; the Double-crested also inhabits inland lakes and large rivers. They dive from the surface of the water to catch fish. As soon as cormorants stop fishing, they go ashore to dry their wings and hold them out to the sun for some time before taking flight. Unlike ducks, their feathers are not completely waterproof. They possess powerful muscles for closing their beaks so they can keep a grip on their prey. When swimming

Great Cormorant

underwater, cormorants hold their wings slightly out from their sides and use their webbed feet to propel themselves forward.

ANHINGAS *(Anhingidae)*

These birds, only one species of which is found in the United States, are similar to the cormorants (see above) but have no hooked bill and their body is more attenuated. Like cormorants they spread their wings to dry. They hunt underwater; many swim with only their head and necks showing. They spear fish with their long, finely serrated bills.

FRIGATEBIRDS *(Fregatidae)*

These are large seabirds with a long wingspan that makes them excellent fliers. They are rarely seen onshore. Frigatebirds have a forked tail and long, hooked bill. They chase and harass other birds forcing them to drop their prey of fish. The male is all black with an orange throat pouch which he inflates during courtship. They are rare wanderers on both coasts.

HERONS *(Ardeidae)*

Great Blue Heron

These are wading birds with long necks and legs, and a measured walk. In hunting, they stalk or wait patiently, then abruptly thrust their head forward to spear prey. Their bills are stout, long and pointed; they feed on fish, frogs and aquatic insects. Herons occupy seacoasts, streams, marshes, ponds and other watery habitats. They fly with their necks folded back in an S-shape, which distinguishes them in flight from the cranes. Herons and egrets often stand hunched with their necks pulled in. At the turn of the century, the egrets were endangered by feather hunters who killed the birds for their breeding plumes.

IBISES and SPOONBILLS *(Threskiornithidae)*
This is another group of birds with characteristics common to the waders: long legs, necks, and bills. The ibises have bills that curve down; the spoonbills have wide flattened bills. They inhabit coasts, marshes, and swamps; and are often brightly colored. Unlike the heron family, birds in this group fly with their legs and necks outstretched.

STORKS *(Ciconiidae)*
These are very large, long-legged birds somewhat like the cranes. Their long, thick bills curve down at the tip. They live along marshes and lagoons and eat fish, rodents, crustaceans and frogs. Storks appear almost like vultures with their bare faces and heads. Their flight is slow and they often soar in circles.

FLAMINGOS *(Phoenicopteridae)*
Members of this family possess a rounded body with a long slender neck and thin, wading legs. Their bizarre bill, which bends abruptly downward in the middle, is used for sifting aquatic animals from shallow pools and lagoons. A native of the Carribean, the Greater Flamingo occasionally wanders north to South Florida. Most flamingos seen elsewhere in the United States are escaped zoo birds.

SWANS, GEESE and DUCKS *(Anatidae)*
This is a large family. Together, they are called waterfowl and, despite variations in size, plumage and habitat, share certain

Blue-winged Teal

common characteristics. They have four toes, the front ones webbed, the hind one slightly elevated and free. Ducks feed from the water's surface, while geese usually feed on land. All have spatulate, blunt bills with serrated comb-like edges. When feeding, their rectangular, fleshy tongue is raised against the palate to squeeze out water through the bill, leaving solid food in the mouth. Waterfowl are strong fliers. In migration, geese and swans often fly in a V-formation. The ducks include many species broken down into subcategories: the dabbling ducks, stiff-tailed ducks, whistling-ducks, perching ducks, pochards, eiders, sea ducks and mergansers. Various imported waterfowl that have escaped from private collections or been released can be found in city parks. Consult a field guide or checklist to find specific representatives of the family that you might see.

AMERICAN VULTURES *(Cathartidae)*

Turkey Vulture

Vultures, sometimes called buzzards, are large dark birds which feed on carrion. They have small, unfeathered heads and strong hooked beaks and possess no talons. Unlike the hawks, vultures can carry nothing away in their feet. They can fly long distances in their search for food and are excellent at soaring. They construct no nests, laying their eggs on ledges and cliffs. Vultures are long-lived birds with small clutches, as is natural in a bird with few enemies. In the early morning they sit around near the roost, sunning themselves until the air currents warm up. Turkey Vultures fly with their wings slightly tilted upwards forming a shallow "V" as they soar overhead. The California Condor, the largest bird in North America, is an endangered species and controlled breeding efforts are being conducted in an effort to expand the population.

KITES, HAWKS and EAGLES *(Accipitridae)*
Keen vision, strongly hooked beaks and sharp talons characterize this family. Included in this group are several subcategories including the accipiter and buteo hawks. The accipiters have short, rounded wings and a long tail. These are the woodland hawks, adept at chasing down smaller birds in flight. The buteos are large soaring hawks which inhabit both woodland and open country. The buteos feed more on ground mammals. Very large, soaring birds, such as the Golden Eagle are also in this family, as are harriers, kites, the Bald Eagle and the Osprey.

Broad-winged Hawk (Buteo)

Sharp-shinned Hawk (Accipiter)

FALCONS and CARACARA *(Falconidae)*
This is another group of predators, distinguished from the previous family by their long, pointed wings that bend at the wrist when they fly. It includes the kestrel, merlin, gyrfalcon and caracara. Like hawks, they have the characteristic bird of prey body designed for power, speed and ability to kill. On the cutting edge of the upper mandible towards the tip is a toothlike projection (absent in caracara) which distinguishes the falcons from other birds of prey. The caracara, a strange mix between a vulture and a falcon has a partially bare head. Falcons have a very rapid wingbeat, almost like a pigeon. They are the fastest fliers in North America. Many falcon species and some accipiters were trained to hunt for sport during the Middle Ages.

Prairie Falcon

CHACHALACAS *(Cracidae)*

Found in scrub along the southern Rio Grande River, there is only one species of this family in the United States. The chachalaca is similar to a turkey, though smaller, and its name is a phonetic interpretation of its call.

GROUSE and PTARMIGAN *(Phasianidae)*

Northern Bobwhite

This family is famliar because many of them are game birds. Inhabiting scrublands, forests and woodlands these are chicken-like birds that dwell on the ground. They have medium-sized, rounded bodies and live on berries, insects, nuts and seeds. Most grouse and prairie-chickens are declining in population and they are difficult to see unless you visit their lek, or breeding grounds.

RAILS, GALLINULES and COOTS *(Rallidae)*

Virginia Rail

Rails are secretive and are heard more often than seen, as they remain hidden in swamps and marshes. Their laterally compressed bodies enable them to pass through small spaces in marsh vegetation, giving rise to the expression "thin as a rail." Since they are poor fliers they will swim in emergencies. Rails have chunky bodies with little, up-turned tails. Gallinules and coots dive and swim; they have frontal shields on their bills. Birds in this family live on aquatic plants, insects, seeds, and frogs. Rails and coots walk and swim with their heads bobbing back and forth. The coot has lobed feet, the others have long toes to support them on the mud.

LIMPKINS *(Aramidae)*

The Limpkin is named for its strange gait which resembles a limp. A wading bird with long neck and bill, it was once hunted almost to extinction. It appears to be making a comeback and can be found in Florida where it feeds on small animals around the edges of swamps and marshes.

CRANES *(Gruidae)*

Cranes are very tall, long-necked birds with drooping, elongated inner secondary feathers that seem to form a "bustle" on their rump. In flight, their necks extend straight out like those of ibises and storks. They inhabit open fields near water and around marshes, and they feed during the day in nearby farmlands. Cranes winter in large flocks in local interior valleys in the Southwest.

PLOVERS *(Charadriidae)*

Plovers are shorebirds found wintering in groups on seacoasts or lakeshores. They are compact, plump birds that run a little, then pause, then run again. Plovers have short, pigeon-like bills, small rounded heads, and large eyes. Some, like the Golden-Plovers and the Black-bellied, breed in the Arctic circle. The Mountain Plover nests in interior grasslands and winters in the Southwest. Many are dusty or sandy colored, and have one or two dark neck bands.

Semipalmated Plover

OYSTERCATCHERS *(Haematopodidae)*

Oystercatchers are well named. Their

large, red-orange bills are flattened allowing them to pry open bivalved mollusks and eat the animal inside. Oystercatchers live on coastal beaches and mudflats; on the West Coast they are found on exposed, rocky seashores.

STILTS and AVOCETS *(Recurvirostridae)*

American Avocet

These are longlegged, graceful waders. Both have very long, slender bills. The avocet's is curved upward; it sweeps its bill sideways while wading through shallow water to capture small aquatic animals. Black-necked Stilts, with their bright pink legs, are found in tidal mudflats or fresh water ponds.

JACANAS *(Jacanidae)*

Jacanas live in tropical areas of the world. The Northern Jacana is a rare inhabitant of ponds and marshes in south Texas. They have extraordinarily long toes and toenails, which enable them to walk over floating water plants, where they hunt for insects and small fish. Above the bill they have a frontal shield, similar to the coots and gallinules. They jerk their short tail with each high reaching step.

SANDPIPERS *(Scolopacidae)*

Willet

This numerous shorebird group varies from the tiny Least Sandpiper with its slender bill to the Long-billed Curlew with its long, sickle-like bill. Sandpipers have slender, more tapered bodies and relatively longer legs than plovers. In winter plumage most sandpipers are mottled colors of gray or brown above, with white below. Their bills are used for probing and vary considerably; bill size and shape are diagnostic in identification. Sandpipers nest largely in the Arctic circle. They migrate in huge flocks along the Atlantic, Pacific and Gulf coasts in spring and fall. Sandpipers frequent shores of streams, ponds and lakes, as well as coastal mudflats during migration. Check your field guide or local checklist to find which sandpipers you are likely to find in your area.

GULLS, TERNS, SKUAS and JAEGERS
(Laridae)

All birds in this family are strong flying seabirds. Jaegers and skuas inhabit the open ocean. They are predatory, and often harass other birds, forcing them to disgorge their prey. Gulls and jaegers take two to four years to develop adult plumage. In order to correctly identify them, the birdwatcher must learn the field marks of each year's plumage. Learn the adult plumages of the gull species first. Most immatures appear brownish and mottled. Gulls and jaegers are omnivorous birds and their range is worldwide, though they are mostly found along the coasts. The gull's bill is strong with a slight hook at the end. Jaegers, terns and gulls have the three front toes joined by webbing, the hind toe is small and somewhat elevated. Gulls are larger than terns and have square or rounded tails, while terns usually have forked tails. Terns fly with their bills pointed downwards, diving headfirst into the water to capture fish.

Great Black-backed Gull

Common Tern

AUKS and PUFFINS *(Alcidae)*

The birds in this family are known as the penguins of the north. Like penguins, their legs are set far back on their bodies so they have an upright stance on land. They have short, narrow wings and short tails. Most are black and white and spend their time in the ocean, diving and swimming expertly. Like shearwaters, alcids (a common term for this family) can "fly" with their wings while submerged. They feed on marine animals, and some develop strangely enlarged bills. They have stocky bodies and webbed feet. Murrelets and auklets are usually seen only well away from the mainland. All alcids nest in huge colonies on sea cliffs.

PIGEONS and DOVES *(Columbidae)*

Rock Dove

Doves are generally thought of as the smaller species, and pigeons the larger within this family. These are the only birds that feed their young on milk, which is produced in the lining of their crop. Especially common in cities, these birds eat grains, seeds, garbage and insects. They are plump, full-breasted and strong fliers. The Rock Dove, or common domestic pigeon, was introduced to the United States from Europe, where it has been domesticated and bred since the 4th century B.C. The Rock Dove comes in all sorts of colors due to this selective breeding by man.

PARROTS *(Psittacidae)*

Parrots are not native to the United States now; however, many domesticated birds have escaped and established wild breeding populations. The Carolina Parakeet, now extinct, was once a common native breeder. Inasmuch as they are native to warm, tropical climates these birds are found in similar areas in this country, notably around Miami and Los Angeles.

CUCKOOS, ANIS and ROADRUNNERS
(Cuculidae)

Members of this family in North America consist of three different cuckoos and the ani and the roadrunner. All have long, graduated tails and feet with two toes pointed forward and two pointed backwards. The cuckoos have the habit of shyly slinking through trees and undergrowth. The roadrunner, a large ground-dwelling cuckoo, runs swiftly to pursue its prey of snakes and lizards. The anis have monstrous bills and nest gregariously in restricted ranges in southern Florida and Texas.

Black-billed Cuckoo

BARN OWLS *(Tytonidae)*

There is only one representative of this family in North America, the Common Barn-Owl. Barn Owls differ from typical owls (see below) having proportionately smaller eyes, long, slender legs, and a heart-shaped facial disc. However, their behavior and life style are quite similar to other owls.

OWLS *(Strigidae)*

Owls are night hunters. They pursue their prey with strong claws and sharp, hooked beaks. They have large heads with eyes that look forward. They possess keen eyesight, even though their eyes have limited sideways vision. To compensate for the limitations on their side vision, owls can swivel their heads up to 270 degrees. This facilitates both sight and hearing. Owls hear extremely well; their facial discs aid in collecting sound waves. Also, the asymmetrical shape and placement of their auditory openings help in locating sound waves. Owl feathers are fluffy at the edges, making their flight noiseless. Like some raptors,

Western Screech-Owl

they cannot digest the entire bodies of their prey, so they regurgitate pellets of fur and bone. Their roosts can be found by searching the ground for these pellets. You can also watch for mobbing behavior in crows and songbirds to detect owls perched in daytime. At night, their hoots and hisses are used to identify individual species.

NIGHTJARS *(Caprimulgidae)*

Well camouflaged, nightjars roost on the ground or perch lengthwise on low branches during the day. They are most active in the half-light of early morning or evening, singing and feeding so effectively at dawn and dusk that they can spend the rest of the day and night dozing. Nightjars have wide mouths fringed with "whiskers" for capturing insects. They have large eyes, small bills and short legs. These birds are usually recognized by their distinctive night calls. Nighthawks are sometimes seen swooping for insects even in mid-day, though they are much more frequently spotted at twilight.

SWIFTS *(Apodidae)*

Swifts appear similar to swallows, but they are distinctly different. Swifts fly by moving their wings up and down, not backward and forward. This gives them a characteristic flickering flight. The rigidity of the swift's wing, with its muscles and arm bones all telescoped against the shoulder gives the bird an appearance of a cigar stuck in a bow. Swifts spend their lives in midair; they roost upon cliffs, in chimneys or near waterfalls. They never perch upon trees or wires the way swallows do. Swifts

Vaux's Swift

and hummingbirds are in the same order. Both have long narrow wings and very small feet.

HUMMINGBIRDS *(Trochilidae)*

These are the smallest birds in North America, and occur in the New World only. Their irridescent feathers reflect a variety of bright colors. Hummingbirds use their grooved tongues inside long bills to probe for nectar and small insects in flowers. They also catch insects from the air. Whether they fly upwards, backwards or hover in place, their high metabolism necessitates nearly constant feeding to stay alive. Hummers aggressively defend their territories, which they may establish around feeders. They are also attracted to colorful flowers, particularly red ones. The adult males are identified by brilliant throat feathers (gorgets), which show color in good light. Females and immatures can be quite difficult to identify.

Anna's Hummingbird

TROGONS *(Trogonidae)*

The trogons belong to a tropical family of gorgeous birds which eat fruit and large insects in foliage. About the size of a jay, these beautiful birds have short bills and long tails. The two North American species are found only in the mountains of southeast Arizona.

KINGFISHERS *(Alcedinidae)*

As their name implies, these birds fish for a living. Residing near streams and in coastal areas, they have a large-headed, crested appearance and a rattle-like call. They use their heavy bills for fishing and for digging nesting burrows in creek banks.

Kingfishers hover or perch over the water looking for prey, then plunge into the water to retrieve a struggling fish.

WOODPECKERS *(Picidae)*

Yellow-bellied Sapsucker

Woodpeckers, sapsuckers and flickers are adapted to climbing up the trunks of trees. They have strong claws, and two toes point forward while two point backwards. Their stiff tails provide support for climbing. Woodpeckers' sharp bills chisel insects out of bark and can drill holes into the wood. Their long sticky tongues protrude to capture insects and to eat sap, as well as acorns and seeds. A cushion inside their skull protects their brain from the constant hammering. Some are communal nesters, sharing nesting duties in holes in tree trunks or phone poles. Their undulating flight and loud calls make this family easy to identify.

The following families belong to the order *Passeriformes*. This is the largest order and it includes more than half the world's species of birds. These are the songbirds, and scientists think they are the most highly developed group of birds. They are characterized by a perching foot with four toes at the same level, three in front and one in the rear with a very large claw. In many parts of the country they are also the birds you are most likely to spot.

Birdwatchers and scientists refer to these birds as passerines. In the beginning, it will be very difficult to tell some of these birds apart. Concentrate on identifying families. Learn to tell a wren from a chickadee from a flycatcher. Their behaviors will be a big help in identification. Then you can refine your skills to identify individual species.

TYRANT FLYCATCHERS *(Tyrannidae)*

Flycatchers commonly perch upright on exposed branches to await the appearance of an insect. Upon spotting one they dart out to grab it, then return to the same perch often flicking their tail upon alighting. Most flycatchers have a crested appearance. The small flycatchers in the genus *Empidonax* are extremely difficult to distinguish from each other. Even very experienced birders have trouble telling them apart. Consult a field guide for the distribution and identification of these species. And don't get discouraged!

Greater Pewee

LARKS *(Alaudidae)*

There are only two species of larks in the United States, one of which is introduced. They are dusky, brownish or grayish birds that live on the ground in grasslands and plowed fields. Their hind claw is very elongated. On the ground they walk rather than hop. Larks move in flocks feeding on seeds and insects. On their nesting territory, their song is high and musical, given in flight. In breeding plumage the male Horned Lark has a distinctive head pattern of black horns and a yellow face.

SWALLOWS (Hirundinidae)

Many people confuse swallows with swifts. Swallows have a wider inner wing than swifts and shorter flight feathers, therefore, their wings are wide-based, tapering at the tip. They have very small feet and bills, and spend most of their time on the wing where they catch flying insects in their wide mouths. Flocks will perch in rows on telephone wires or roofs. Most nest in colonies in trees, cliffs or under

Barn Swallow

bridges. At the end of summer they gather in enormous flocks in preparation for early migration south, some as far as South America.

JAYS, CROWS, MAGPIES and RAVENS
(Corvidae)

American Crow

These birds are large for passerines, the ravens being the largest. They are highly visible and vocal birds, and are easy to identify. Crows, as a family, have probably evolved the most intelligence among birds. Jays, crows and magpies are gregarious, loud and aggressive. Crows and ravens are entirely black, while jays and magpies may be brightly colored. All have strong feet and medium-length bills, and are omnivorous.

TITMICE and CHICKADEES *(Paridae)*

Mountain Chickadee

These are small, long-tailed, plump birds that flock together. Their bills are short and pointed. They are weak fliers but are acrobatic in trees and bushes, hopping around and often hanging upside down to feed. Chickadees and titmice are fond of seeds and berries, and can be lured to backyard feeders. Their coloring is grayish and drab.

VERDINS *(Remizidae)*

Verdins are tiny, grayish birds with yellow heads that inhabit the desert and arid scrub vegetation, primarily mesquite and creosote, of the Southwest. They build large, oval nests of thorny twigs with side entrances. They are lively birds similar to the Bushtit. Their bill, unlike that of the Bushtit, is straight-edged and sharply pointed. The two species are seldom found in the same habitat.

BUSHTITS *(Aegithalidae)*

Bushtits are tiny, plump birds of plain, grayish brown reminiscent of a chickadee. They have proportionately long tails. They twitter nervously among themselves as they move from one bush to another foraging for insects. Bushtits are found in oak woodland and chaparral in the West where their nest is an elaborate sack or dome with a side entrance. In the non-breeding season, they travel in loose flocks which often contain other species, such as warblers.

NUTHATCHES *(Sittidae)*

Nuthatches climb down tree trunks head-first, searching for insects and larvae in the bark. They possess short tails and necks, and powerful feet to help in climbing. Often found in flocks with chickadees in winter, nuthatches are blue-gray above and white below. They have woodpecker-like bills and their flight is undulating like that of a miniature woodpecker.

Red-breasted Nuthatch

CREEPERS *(Certhiidae)*

There is only one species of this family in the United States. These small birds are camouflaged with lengthwise brown streaks. They climb up trees, like tiny woodpeckers, but have a slender decurved bill which is used for probing rather than drumming. Creepers are common but hard to see. Listen for their high thin notes in coniferous forests.

BULBULS *(Pycnonotidae)*

The bulbuls are an Old World family of songbirds, medium-sized, that move about actively in noisily chattering musical groups. In 1960 some Red-whiskered Bulbuls escaped from captivity in the Miami area. They now breed there in the wild. They are weak fliers and non-migratory, feeding on fruits and seeds of ornamental plantings.

WRENS *(Troglodytidae)*

Bewick's Wren

Wrens are rotund, little birds, with brownish plumage. Their bills are slender and slightly decurved. Wrens are found near the ground where they feed on insects and spiders. They have a characteristic habit of cocking their short tails straight up which helps in identification. Wrens will respond well to a "pishing" sound and usually come up to a perch to scold the observer. They are excellent vocalists, as well.

DIPPERS *(Cinclidae)*

There is only one species of this family in the United States. Dippers look like large, slate gray wrens, but they have their own unique lifestyle. They wade, swim and dive in rushing mountain streams. They can even walk underwater feeding on aquatic insects and small fish. In high mountain streams, watch for this gray bird bobbing and dipping on the rocks.

THRUSHES, KINGLETS and GNAT-CATCHERS *(Muscicapidae)*

American Robin

This is a very diverse group, including many common songbirds. The thrush group, which includes robins, bluebirds, and solitaires as well as other thrushes, shares a distinctive silhouette with slim bill, erect posture and rather long legs. They all have spotted young. The thrushes are some of the world's finest singers. Kinglets and gnatcatchers are small birds either with whitish wingbars or bluish-gray upperparts. They have very slender, pointed black bills. Kinglets are the tiniest of all passerines in the United States. Wrentits, in a unique subfamily of their own, are year-round residents of coastal chaparral in the West.

MOCKINGBIRDS, THRASHERS and CATBIRDS *(Mimidae)*

Northern Mockingbird

Birds in this category are recognized as outstanding songsters throughout the United States. Many can mimic the calls of other birds and animals. All have strong bills, most curve down. Their plumage is primarily gray or brown, and they some-times hold their long tails up in a slightly cocked position. They feed on insects, seeds, berries and fruit. The various western species of thrashers are found in specific habitats only.

PIPITS and WAGTAILS *(Motacillidae)*

These birds live on the ground and, like the larks, have elongated hind claws. Many pump their tails up and down when they walk. Pipits have thin warbler-like bills with streaked sparrow-like bodies. In winter they flock in open fields and beaches. Wagtails are rare breeders in Alaska and rare visitors to the rest of the United States.

WAXWINGS *(Bombycillidae)*

Waxwings are characterized by crests on their heads and yellow tips on their tails. Their plumage is silky. They have short bills and feed on insects and berries. They flock to bushes of ripening berries and sometimes feed until they can barely fly.

PHAINOPEPLAS (or SILKY FLYCAT-CHERS) *(Ptilogonatidae)*

The Phainopepla resembles the waxwings, but its crest is more erect and ragged. It is only found in the Southwest. In flight it displays white flashes on its wings. It feeds on insects caught in flight, and on berries. The adult male is shiny black.

SHRIKES *(Laniidae)*

Shrikes don't behave like typical passerines. They are more hawk-like, with strong, hooked bills. From overlooking perches they dive down on insects, rodents, lizards or other birds. They have earned the common name of "butcher birds" because, lacking talons, they often impale their prey on thorns or barbed wire. At first glance, they resemble the mockingbird.

Northern Shrike

STARLINGS *(Sturnidae)*

European Starling

This is an Old World family, two species of which have been introduced to North America. The Crested Myna is fairly common near Vancouver, British Columbia. The European Starling, however, is the only species common throughout. Starlings, with their glossy black plumage and yellow bill, can drive out native species in competition for nest holes.

VIREOS *(Vireonidae)*

Vireos are small songbirds with short, somewhat heavy bills with a slight hook at the tip. They are often confused with warblers or *Empidonax* flycatchers. Some vireos have "spectacles" and wingbars, others have "eyebrows" and no wingbars. They are all olive, gray, or dusky yellow. They are not as active and busy as warblers, nor do they perch upright as do the flycatchers. To distinguish them from the wood warblers, look for relatively sluggish movement through the vegetation and loud, phrased songs. They feed on insects.

Yellow-throated Vireo

SPARROWS *(Emberizidae)*

This is a very large family, the members of which are thought to be related in an evolutionary sense, although these similarities are not always obvious to the eye. Common birds in this group include warblers, waterthrushes, tanagers, grosbeaks, cardinals, buntings, sparrows, towhees, juncos, longspurs, blackbirds and orioles. Their bills, plumage and habitats vary so much that we will break them down into subfamilies to help you identify these abundant passerines.

Wood Warblers *(Parulinae)*

These tiny birds are often yellow, olive, or gray and accented with brilliant spots of color, usually in the male's plumage. The females and immatures are difficult to identify, so go carefully. Warblers, with their tiny, needle-like bills, are usually found searching the undersides of leaves high in woodland trees. They flitter from branch to twig, catching insects. Called the "butterflies of the bird world," they are a challenge to catch in your binoculars. Warblers have energetic and pleasing songs, distinctive enough to be useful aids in identification. Most warblers are highly migratory,

Yellow-rumped Warbler

spending only spring and summer in the United States. Arrival of these brilliant birds is a spring event in the East, when birdwatchers hope to spot them before deciduous trees obscure the warblers with new growth.

Tanagers *(Thraupinae)*

Summer Tanager

Tanagers are medium-sized songbirds found high in conifers or large shade trees. The males are brightly colored, usually lemon yellow or red. The females and immatures, on the other hand, are dull olive and green. Like the orioles, tanagers feed on nectar and fruit but their bills are heavier and less tapered than the orioles. They are fond of catching bees!

Cardinals, Grosbeaks and Buntings *(Cardinalinae)*

Northern Cardinal

Cardinals and grosbeaks are very similar to finches. They have over-sized stubby bills that are wide at the base and curve sharply toward the tip. The males are colorful, the females duller. All these birds consume insects, fruit and seeds. Buntings prefer weedy fields and open country. They are difficult to tell from finches.

Towhees, Sparrows and Longspurs *(Emberizinae)*

Rufous-sided Towhee

This group includes medium-sized sparrows known as towhees; the true sparrows, which are usually small, grayish-brown and streaked; and the longspurs which are found in open country. These all feed on seeds, grubs and insects and live in low bushes or near the ground. In spring, the males will sing from conspicuous perches. Except for the longspurs, male and female plumages are alike; however, juvenile plumages are different from the adults.

Blackbirds and Orioles *(Icterinae)*
The birds in this group (except for the bobolink) have slender bills with sharp points. Compared to the finches, they have longer and slimmer bodies with longer tails. This is a disparate group, and includes the gregarious blackbirds and grackles who congregate in huge flocks and walk around on the ground; orioles which are found high in the trees, often weaving elaborate hanging nests; the cowbird who lays her eggs in other bird's nests; and the meadowlarks found singing melodiously in grassy fields.

Scott's Oriole

FINCHES *(Fringillidae)*
These are the true finches resembling the familiar canary. Finches are small to medium-sized birds that often frequent backyard feeders. They have plump bodies, notched tails, and conical bills for cracking seeds. In the winter, finches migrate in flocks. Goldfinches and siskins like thistles.

Lesser Goldfinch

WEAVERS *(Passeridae)*
These are Old World birds. Two species live in the United States. The Eurasian Tree Sparrow is common only near St. Louis. The House Sparrow, also known as the English Sparrow, is universally abundant in cities throughout the United States. House Sparrows don't sing, they have a loud series of *"chirps."* Both birds resemble native sparrows, but they have thicker bills. They feed on insects and seeds. The male House Sparrow is more striking than the drab female.

House Sparrow

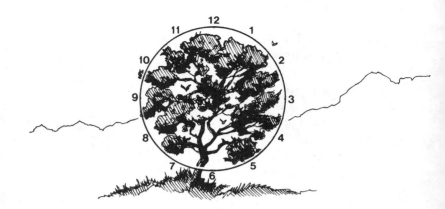

5. The Field Trip

Everything covered in this book so far has been designed to prepare you for the exciting moment when you embark on your first field trip. No matter how many guide books you read or song tapes you listen to, there is no substitute for days spent outdoors looking at birds in a variety of habitats.

The crisp sunshine and still air, the murmuring of sparrows in a hedgerow, a meadowlark whistling on a fencepost, and there you are—absorbing it all as you amble leisurely along. The essence of birdwatching is the pure enjoyment of being there. Do not become discouraged if you miss a bird, or cannot narrow one down to the correct species. The chief ingredient of a successful bird outing is always the participant's enthusiasm. One word of warning: the thrill of birding is addictive. After your first field trip, consider yourself hooked!

This chapter will concern itself with the basic field trip skills you need in order to approach birds and study them in nature. We have included also a sample birdwalk in the East and one in the West, complete with typical birds you might see.

CLOTHING AND EQUIPMENT

The best time to prepare for a bird trip is the night before. An early start in the morning is important, so organize your clothing and equipment in advance. Proper clothing requirements for birdwatching are highly flexible and depend upon the individual, the weather and the destination of the trip. Find out beforehand as much as you can about weather conditions, the nature of the terrain and the length of the outing.

In winter, in cold and rainy conditions, birding can be positively miserable if you lack adequate warm clothing. You may stand for hours, often in exposed areas and without the warming effects of strenuous exercise. Wool hats covering the ears, mittens or gloves, heavy parkas, warm pants, long underwear and wool socks are all welcome gear. Stick to subdued colors in your outer garments; birds can be distracted by bright clothing. Rainy weather calls for water-repellent anoraks or waterproof jackets. Some modern fabrics, such as "Gore-tex" claim to minimize condensation that occurs in other outerwear. In any case, the importance of staying warm and dry in winter birding conditions cannot be overemphasized.

In summer, a good sunscreen and hat are essential. Also, insect repellent is a must in infested areas during spring and summer. Meadows and bogs and inland lakes are excellent for birding during those seasons, because the birds feed on the mosquitoes. But you do not want them, and other biting or stinging insects, feeding on you!

At any time of year, proper footgear will increase your enjoyment of your hours in the field. High-top hiking boots, or low cut walking shoes made of leather are preferable. The porosity of the leather allows for some ventilation of your feet. However, many people choose to wear canvas athletic shoes. In any case, durable and comfortable shoes are important. Obviously, the quality of the terrain will vary from trip to trip, and will affect your choice of shoes. For instance, in the desert thornproof shoes are a necessity. Be prepared before you leave the house.

Many birders carry a pair of rubber boots or waders in their car at all times. These knee or hip boots are indispensable for wading in shallow creek beds, walking through wet meadows, or stalking shorebirds on mudflats. However, rubber boots are not advisable for day to day wear, because they keep your feet too airtight. Obtain a pair at some point to avoid the distinct annoyance of cold, wet feet distracting you no matter how thrilling the birding. Rubber boots are often available at army surplus outlets at a minimal price, or you can find them at sporting goods stores or in mail-order catalogs.

Gather your necessary equipment together the night before; you will find a day pack is useful to consolidate items. A typical list of what you will need for a field trip includes: your field guide, notebook and regional checklist, spotting scope, insect repellent, lip balm, waterproof boots and binoculars. Always walk out the door with your binoculars hanging around your neck. That way you will never leave them behind!

There is still one important item to be mentioned: snacks. You will be amazed at the ravenous hunger one develops during bird outings; perhaps it is the fresh air or the stimulation of seeing all those great birds. If you get up at 5:00 A.M., you can be sure you will want a mid-morning snack at 8:00, and by 10:00 you very well may be ready for lunch. Tuck in plenty of nourishing, portable snacks because you don't know where you may find yourself when hunger pangs strike. Also, find out if you should bring your own water. Unfortunately, many otherwise delightful streams contain undrinkable water.

WEATHER

What about weather? If it looks like rain or wind, should you cancel and stay home? Not necessarily. It is true strong, windy conditions make land birds difficult to spot amongst the swaying leaves and branches. Also, most perching birds tend to hide out and stay put during high winds. But if you are looking at water birds, or out on the open ocean, wind does not affect the birding as much. Shorebirds, waterfowl and pelagic birds can get by on cold blustery days, and often will drop down to rest for protection. For example, on the eastern seacoast, a brisk gale out of the northeast could blow in rare alcids. On the west coast, a northwest wind might blow pelagic birds closer to shore. Hawks, especially during migration, seem to react to temperature drops and winds from certain directions by migrating over the mountain ridges of the eastern United States in great flocks.

Rain, unless it is pouring down in torrents, is no cause for discouragement. Birds often move around searching for food during, or right after, a light drizzle or brief shower. With proper clothing, wet weather can be a challenge, and it may keep the birds down. If the birds are stopping off during migration, bad weather may induce them to stay, thereby allowing you to view them before they fly on after the storm. For example, birders on the California coast know that a light drizzle or morning fog can ground such migrants as vagrant warblers, which become disoriented and drop in to perch. On the Gulf Coast of Texas, the same phenomenon occurs when a weather front grounds the migrating landbirds on their way north from Central America. Thus, unusual birds are often observed on cloudy, drizzly days.

Ideal birding weather is a calm day with a high overcast, reducing the glare of the sun. Birds stay active longer into the morning when it is cool and cloudy. On warm and sunny days, bird life tends to subside by mid-morning.

TIME OF DAY

What is the best time of day to observe birds? Early morning and late afternoon are when songbirds feed most actively. However, early morning, especially the three or four hours after dawn, is by far the most desirable time. Going out before dawn, especially in springtime, will expose you to the dawn chorus and give you a chance to listen to bird songs, though at first it may be too dark to see the birds themselves. In the late afternoon, land birds are again feeding before they retire for the night. Although never as profitable as early morning birding, this can be a beautiful time of day to get out.

Other kinds of birds are easily visible throughout the whole day. Shorebirds and water birds are examples, particularly in migration. Large birds of prey, such as hawks and vultures, are best observed after mid-morning when they soar on warm air currents while scanning for prey. This is convenient for the birdwatcher. A field trip can commence with viewing perching birds in the early morning, then proceed to hawk watching around mid-day, and conclude with some hours spent at shorebird or water bird habitats later when time of day is not important.

Some birds are best searched for after dark. At twilight, or shortly thereafter, it is fun to drive back roads on summer evenings listening for poorwills, whip-poor-wills or night-hawks. Later, a couple of hours past sunset or before dawn, birders use flashlights and taped owl calls to observe owls.

Whatever the time of day, you should be aware of the position of the sun while you are birdwatching. Try to view birds with the sun behind you. Naturally, this cannot always be achieved. But, it is frustrating to study birds while looking into the sun; their color and markings are obscured and it is difficult to see any details. Therefore, in planning outings, keep in mind the sun's position to minimize the glare. Late afternoon is a perfect time to view shorebirds with the sun at your back. It is disastrous with the sun glancing off tidal mudflats and straight into your eyes.

GETTING CLOSE TO BIRDS IN THE FIELD

When you are birding in the field, you should try to approach as closely as possible to the bird you wish to study, without disturbing it. Birds are easily startled by sudden movements and loud noises, and will undoubtedly fly away before you can get your binoculars up! However, there are techniques you can learn to get quite close to birds without frightening them.

Let us say you are on foot, walking through a woodland area of tall trees and undergrowth. First, you will want to move very cautiously. Keep sudden body movements to a minimum. Never point or wave your arms. Raise and lower your binoculars slowly. You should go forward carefully, scanning nearby trees and bushes for every movement. Watch where you put your feet, a snapping twig or loud splash can scare a bird.

As you stalk a bird, it is better to approach from the side, or indirectly, rather than straight forward. The bird is less likely to flush if you approach gradually; you may even crouch low to minimize your visibility on the skyline. Meanwhile, listen and look, don't talk. Songbirds are located by sound as frequently as by movement. Listen for chips and calls and try to locate the bird uttering them. If you are chatting to your companions throughout the field trip, you will miss most of the birdlife.

At last! You have spotted a wiggling branch on a nearby alder tree. A bird hops into view. Always look for the bird with your naked eye first; then locate it through your binoculars.

Some people seem to possess sharper eyes than others. This is indeed a talent, but the ability to spot birds can improve with practice. To speed up your reaction time, try clasping your hands lightly around your binoculars, or keeping them partially raised, so you can bring them up to your eyes without losing the bird in view. When you have seen the bird's movement, make a quick mental note of its position, then—not taking your eyes off it—raise the binoculars.

Frequently you will want to describe the bird's position in the foliage in front of you, so your companions can share your find. It is important to do this as accurately and quickly as possible. Knowing the names of common plants and trees in your part of the country is invaluable in pinpointing bird locations. "It's in that green bush over there," does not tell us much. Whereas, "It's on the righthand side of the tallest sycamore tree in front of us, halfway up at about 3 o'clock" tells exactly where the bird is located.

Birders have found it helpful to superimpose an imaginary clock face on the tree or bush they are describing, and the "time" on that clock is the bird's exact position. Thus, a bird in the top center of the tree is at 12 o'clock, one to the left and halfway down is at 9 o'clock, and so forth. This can be helpful on pelagic trips too, if you designate the bow of the boat as 12 o'clock. You will notice field trip leaders and teachers using the clock face technique frequently to show others the birds they have found.

You now have your binoculars focused on the bird. But it looks very unfamiliar, perhaps a species you have never encountered until today. The possibility this may be a life bird makes your heart leap! Try to stay calm. Look at the bird as long and as carefully as possible. Do not rush to fumble through your field guide. Many experts advise against taking field guides out with you at all, maintaining you should check your field notes against them only after returning home. If you must tote your guide, refrain from looking at it until you have noticed the silhouette, head and bill, field marks and behavior of the bird in question. Do this out loud if you have a friend with you. The friend can then take notes on your oral description. A small pocket notebook or mini-recorder is useful for this. If you take time to look in your book, the bird may fly away before you have really examined it and noted the key identification marks.

FURTHER TIPS

Further field trip hints are listed below. Use them the next time you go out.

• If you are looking at birds high up in tall trees, use the slope of the hill to get on their level as much as possible. That is, if you are walking along a bank or steep slope, the tops of trees growing further downslope will be at eye level for you, thereby eliminating the stiff neck syndrome. This works well in coniferous and deciduous forests where the birds are high up and the trees stand close together.

• If you are using a telescope, scan the area first with your binoculars. For instance, when birding a swampy section for distant waders, use the binoculars first before actually zeroing in with the scope on an individual bird. Once you have the bird spotted, use various landmarks as guides and attempt to focus your scope on the bird.

• In spring and fall, when birds are moving about the countryside a great deal, stay put in one spot and observe the activity around you. Sit down in a comfortable place: on a rock, by a stream, or even on your own patio or porch. If you remain very still, the birds will soon resume their search for food and go about their business fearlessly in your presence. In spring and early summer, you will view the territorial struggles and hear the vocal performances of nesting birds. In fall, roving bands of migrants or flocks of winter visitors make fascinating birdwatching. In fact, birdwatching from a specific location season after season, accompanied by good notetaking, is one of the most scientifically meaningful exercises the amateur can undertake.

• Be aware of "edge" situations when you go out birding. The greatest numbers of birds are found where two or three habitats intersect. For example, if you are watching a meadow, try to position yourself on the edge, where a forested section borders it. Better yet, if a creek or pond is nearby, you can sit on the edge of the meadow and observe it, the forest and the water environment as well. You will see birds flying back and forth, maybe to hunt in the meadow and roost in the forest.

Or, birds will be drinking and bathing in the creek, then flying into the meadow to feed on weeds and thistles.

• Cars and boats can act as blinds from which to watch birds. A slow-moving vehicle is not as startling to birds as the human form. If you remain in the car, you can approach quite closely to wintering flocks of sparrows sitting on fence lines, raptors hunting from telephone poles and other birds using roadside perches. Cars are especially convenient in winter when they form a cozy blind from which to study birds without the discomfort of freezing weather. You can take very good field notes under these conditions, especially when warmed by a hot cup of coffee.

Boats, too, are excellent for observing birds on lakes or the open ocean. Of course, pelagic trips owe their success to this factor. Rowboats and canoes are also a good way to get close to birds on freshwater lakes and streams. If you have access to a boat, you can enjoy approaching grebes, herons, ducks, osprey and kingfishers in this manner.

• You will notice some birds, like people, can show individual variations within the species. There will be certain Song Sparrows that look scruffy, or certain male House Finches that are very pale orange or you may come across an albino form of a species. Some birds do not look exactly like the picture in the field guide, yet they are not another species. For example, that scruffy Song Sparrow may not show the dark spot in the center of his breast. If all the other marks for that species check out correctly, it could be this particular sparrow has just had a bath, or his feathers may have arranged themselves so as not to form a spot. When studying hawks, you may hear the terms "dark phase" and "light phase." These are individual variations within the species and simply mean one individual bird may have very dark plumage while another is very light. However, they both would be the same kind of bird, e.g. Red-tailed Hawk. It takes practice to learn when these differences mean a new species, and when they are slight individual variations. The more familiar you become with birds in the field, the easier it is to pick out new species.

• Do not be intimidated by birders with more expertise than you. After your first few field trips, you will begin to encounter individuals who have been birdwatching for a number of years. Remember, they were beginners once, too. Do not hesitate to ask questions, no matter how simple they appear. Top-notch birders are thrilled to have an eager beginner in the group. And, use your notebook to jot down pertinent tips.

• At first, the number of new facts may seem overwhelming. Do not let this deter you. Every time you go out into the field with a leader expect to retain 20% of what you have seen and heard. This really is quite a lot, you can never absorb all of it at one time.

• Develop your own mnemonic devices to associate with difficult bird identification problems. This may sound silly, but we have found it quite successful. Thus, a short phrase or word can be the key to recalling important field marks or characteristics. For example, when looking at Elegant and Royal Terns in winter plumage remember, "Royal has the eye out of the black, Elegant's is in the black." Emphasizing the letter "l" can help in sandpiper identifiation, for example, "the Least Sandpiper has light legs." "The Downy descends" refers to the descending whinny of the Downy Woodpecker. "Hooded Oriole has no hood" points out the lack of black on the Hooded Oriole's head. "Cooper's contrasts" refers to the contrasting head and back of a Cooper's Hawk, which will differentiate it from the uniform color of the head and back of a Sharp-shinned Hawk. You can create your own phrases this way and it will help you retain important facts.

• Although you will want to participate in bird classes, keep in mind that birdwatching by yourself has a quality of peace and concentration you can never duplicate in a group. The bird you laboriously puzzle over and identify yourself will not soon be forgotten. The solitude of birding alone allows you to escape to a world removed, and provides a wonderful challenge to the intellect.

ATTRACTING BIRDS BY SOUND

As birders walk slowly through wooded areas, parks or gardens, they often stop and utter a sound like "pish, pish, pish" or "spshsh, spshsh, spshsh." This may seem peculiar to a beginner, but it is a way of stirring up songbirds so they scold the intruder or perch nearby to investigate. For some reason, this noise arouses the curiosity of certain birds. Other kinds of birds are markedly unmoved by it. Sparrows, wrens, chickadees, nuthatches and some warblers are very responsive. Once one bird begins scolding, it may be joined by other small birds in a mobbing action. Birds may even fly over your head to regard you from a closer perch. Others will simply jump up or move about enough to let you spot them. Obviously, this technique is hopeless on waders, shorebirds or raptors. It is definitely worth trying, from time to time, with most songbirds.

There are other methods of stirring up songbirds so you can lure them out of hiding for study. In the East, the call of the Eastern Screech-Owl, and in the West, the call of the Northern Pygmy-Owl can elicit a mobbing reaction from warblers and other small birds. They become alerted to what they assume is an owl's presence, and will attempt to drive it away. Many birdwatchers learn to imitate these owl calls themselves. If you cannot manage the calls yourself, you can bring tapes of them into the field. This can be a very effective technique for attracting birds, but should be used judiciously and with a sense of ethics. Birds are very sensitive to territorial threats, especially during the nesting season, and can be driven from an area by overuse of tapes. Also, responding to owl calls uses up precious energy in small birds, energy that takes extra food and time to replace.

Some birders pose a serious threat by indiscriminately playing taped calls to attract birds. Male birds, when hearing the song of another male of the same species, will become antagonized and may abandon nesting efforts or leave the territory. In heavily birded areas, such as southeastern Arizona, the habitats are severely restricted and only a limited number of birds can exist. The use of tapes in such a fragile ecosystem is very detrimental. For example, the use of tapes to attract the famed Elegant Trogon has resulted in such harrassment of the trogons that all taping devices have been banned on their breeding grounds in Arizona. Elsewhere, used judiciously, tapes or human imitations of owl calls can be used to a birdwatcher's benefit when it has been determined that no long term damage will result.

You are now equipped to handle your first birdwalk or field trip. We repeat: the beauty and wonder of birds is everywhere. You do not need excursions to faraway places. Just walk out your front door and turn down the street to the nearest park.

The two birdwalks described below are designed to show you some typical spring breeding birds you might encounter in a local park in two very different regions of the United States. The first covers a suburban neighborhood in upper New York state. The second account takes you on a birdwalk in a lowland section of the California coast. We will mention a representative sampling of ten birds common to the two sections of the country. Some of these birds will be found in both areas, such as the Downy Woodpecker and the Yellow Warbler. Others, like the Red-eyed Vireo in the East and the Bushtit in the West, are unique to their region. Using the field trip skills already discussed, let's ramble through two imaginary areas and see what birds we can discover and identify.

Before beginning our walk, we will look at a regional checklist to ascertain all the breeding birds that nest in that particular habitat. These will be the most abundant birds in springtime. Our imaginary walks do not include migrant birds which might be pausing on their journey to more northerly climates. But, on a real walk we would familiarize ourselves with species migrating at this time of year because we could reasonably expect to see some. All this information is available on checklists issued by local bird clubs.

Walking slowly, binoculars poised, you are ready to enter this woodland tract with a sense of anticipation. Will you be able to identify any of those birds that, up until now, you never really noticed? Will you succeed in hearing a bird call and actually be able to locate the bird through your binoculars?

Come and see how easy birdwatching can be.

AN EASTERN BIRDWALK

It is a warm morning in mid-May, the leaves are covering the trees with a fine, green mist and a park near your house looks promising as a place to test your new birdwatching knowledge. The park contains many deciduous hardwood trees and a lush tangle of undergrowth.

As soon as the entrance gate clangs softly behind you, a loud "*jay, jay, jay*" greets the world from the beech tree overhead. Immediately, the harsh-voiced call attracts your attention. It does not take long before a couple of large, blue birds with crests come bounding down, branch by branch, to investigate. They are so close you hardly need binoculars to spot the white patches on their wings and tail. The vivid azure of the birds' plumage, combined with their aggressive behavior, make these birds easier to recognize than many others. They are Blue Jays. Even a nonbirder notices the jay's noisy habits. Your first bird identification problem turns out to be a fairly simple one.

This pair of Blue Jays will assume a quiet, more secretive manner as they undertake nesting responsibilities later in the spring. Their reputation as thieves of the eggs and young of other birds has been established, although somewhat exaggerated. In fall and winter, you will observe Blue Jays congregating in noisy flocks to search for food. When a group of jays locates an owl dozing in the daylight hours, they will unmercifully tease it by screaming and diving at it. Crows, members of the same family, will mob owls too. The birdwatcher can benefit from these mobbing displays and can often catch a glimpse of roosting owls and hawks. Sometimes jays flush out other rare or difficult to spot birds by their actions.

At the moment, these showoffs are announcing your presence to the whole park.

Blue Jay

The path ahead meanders through undergrowth, down a slope toward a small stream. Stopping frequently to watch for movement, you proceed. A twig on a near bush wiggles slightly, and you raise your binoculars in time to view a small, brownish bird as it dives across the path, tail pumping away in a weak flight pattern. But wait…it is now hiding at the base of some grasses, hopping about on the ground. A good guess would be a sparrow of some kind. That tail-pumping action in flight is important. As the bird turns toward you at last, you observe a conical bill, black and brown head stripings and the chunky little body of a sparrow. The fine, dark streaks on its light breast tend to form a blotch in the middle, a good field mark for the Song Sparrow.

Song Sparrows, one of the most widely distributed birds in the United States, are fond of just this sort of habitat: tangled vegetation in parks and gardens, near water if possible. Their cheerful call, as rendered by Thoreau, "*Maids! Maids! Maids! Hang up your teakettle-ettle-ettle,*" is one of the first bird songs you should learn, whether you bird in the East or West.

Meanwhile, a fussy racket is issuing from a pile of dead wood behind you. What makes such a buzzing, scolding call? You stop and turn, anxious to track down the culprit. Catching a glimpse of the bird, you should focus on the silhouette first. This is easy! The cocked tail and small size of the bird indicate a member of the wren family. Noting the brown underparts, lack of any prominent field marks, and the finely barred brown tail, you decide, correctly, that it is a House Wren. Other North American wrens, except the tiny Winter Wren, would have exhibited a prominent white eye stripe, while this bird did not. The House Wren's spring song is an effervescent warble. When singing, wrens often do not cock their tail, but tuck it straight down and under. Wren behavior and silhouette is so distinctive you can usually recognize them right away.

House Wren

Song Sparrow

Before moving on down the path, notice the bird outlined against the morning sky atop a bayberry bush at 12 o'clock. The bird is about the size of a robin, but totally different in overall shape. It has a long tail that hangs straight down and its head is held high as it sings in short, loud phrases. You look at the head and bill shape, observing a slight curvature to the thin, long bill. It reminds you of a mockingbird. But you can see no color on the bird, because of the sun's glare. Mentally sifting through other birds that might be in the mockingbird family, you come to the thrashers. How about a Brown Thrasher? From the checklist you already know this is the common thrasher in your area. Indeed, it is a Brown Thrasher, singing its spring territorial proclamation. When the Brown Thrasher finally moves, you are able to see the reddish-brown head and back, and the dark-streaked, whitish underparts. Here is a perfect situation for practicing silhouettes when plumage details are hard to view. Rely on your knowledge of characteristic family silhouettes, always noting the bill shape.

Brown Thrasher

You are about to stroll further, when you become aware of a loud, emphatic song continuing monotonously in the background. As the bird approaches, you try to follow the sound, looking for any movement above. It must be high up, hidden by the leaves. Over and over the bird is repeating short, deliberate segments of its spring song. The segments often end with a rising inflection. It is so difficult to see this bird! Focusing in on the twinkling leaves, you finally spot a small, gray bird with a black-bordered, white eye stripe and an olive-green back. It is warbler-sized, but the bill appears thicker, unlike the pencil thin bill of a wood warbler. Also, the bird moves about sluggishly whereas most wood warblers are nervously active. Could it be a kind of vireo? As you watch, it slowly raises its blue-gray crown plumage, perhaps in concern at your presence. It has no wing bars. You conclude it is a Red-eyed Vireo. Unless you can get very close to the bird, the red eye itself is difficult to see. Red-eyes are the abundant vireo of eastern deciduous woods. A Warbling Vireo, another possibility, would be smaller and paler with no black line above the white eyebrow. In pinpointing this bird, your first clue was the loud, measured song. The second was the size of the bird and the shape of its bill.

Red-eyed Vireo

The path towards the creek is worth scanning as you move forward down the slope. The woods are teeming with birdlife this morning. Everywhere you feel the presence of birds hunting for food and establishing nesting territories. The undulating flight of what must be a woodpecker suddenly crosses the path and the bird lands on a decaying tree trunk in a clearing. It begins drumming away at the bark. Watching the woodpecker, you observe its small size, white back and short bill. There are two common woodpeckers of the northeast that show an elongated white patch on the back: the Hairy and the Downy. With experience, the relative size of these two becomes obvious through your binoculars. The Downy Woodpecker is two inches smaller than the Hairy, and has a shorter, more slender bill. Also, the Downy shows black bars on the white, outer tail feathers whereas the Hairy's are all white.

At the moment, the Downy Woodpecker has vanished into a small hole in the trunk. Later his head protrudes, highlighted by a red patch on the crown, signifying a male bird. Downy Woodpeckers are less shy than the look-alike Hairy Woodpecker. The former frequent backyard feeders in winter. The small size of the Downy enables it to occasionally hang from the thinner outer branches of trees, whereas the Hairy sticks to the sturdier trunks. The call of the Downy is a rattling, descending whinny. Members of the woodpecker family are easy to recognize, but arriving at the correct species takes some scrutiny of more detailed field marks.

Downy Woodpecker

Northern Cardinal ♀

Scanning the path ahead, you see a mystery bird fly in. It is olive-gray with dull, reddish wings and pinkish underparts. You look at the head first. Its crown consists of a tufted crest. The bird possesses a heavy, conical bill, like the grosbeaks. The oversized bill, combined with the unmistakable crest, point to a member of the *Emberizidae* family. The only possible eastern bird with a conspicuous crest like this one is a Northern Cardinal. Thus, even before this dull, female cardinal is joined by its brilliant scarlet mate, you have succeeded in figuring out the correct species. Cardinals remain paired throughout the year, and both male and female are accomplished vocalists. Of course, the male's red color is so spectacular you could identify him at once. When looking at the female, however, your knowledge of bird silhouettes was invaluable in narrowing it to the family.

By now, streamside vegetation is prominent. Scattered small willows are growing by the water. It is tough to sort out the birds hiding in the thick foliage. However, a flash of bright yellow is its own announcement! This time you are not able to view the whole bird at once. Try to glimpse the head. By the size of the bird, it may be a warbler.

You decide to attempt to "pish" it out. The warbler responds to your call by moving close enough for a better look. The tiny, thin bill is perfect for a warbler silhouette, and it has a dark eye set in an all-yellow head, a key field mark for the Yellow Warbler. Also, the whole bird appears yellow, with faint reddish streakings on the breast. These field marks all add up to a male Yellow Warbler. Females and males in fall plumage lack the chestnut streakings, but the black eye set against the pale yellow head is always reliable. To practice learning bird songs, you stop and listen: "*sweet, sweet, sweet, I'm so sweet.*" It is a loud, rapid crescendo of notes, and a good first warbler song to commit to memory.

Yellow Warbler ♂

Arriving at the water's edge, you look up and down the stream in either direction. The availability of water is a lure to all birds; even those species that regularly inhabit drier areas will visit the stream for bathing and drinking. You count two more of the now-familiar Song Sparrows, skulking near the bank and picking up morsels in the mud. Another pair of House Wrens are busily chattering to each other, playing around the end of a dead stump. No doubt they are scouting a possible nesting site.

You scan the tops of the taller trees growing along the stream, detecting movement in the very top of that oak opposite. All at once, a medium-sized bird emerges from the dense foliage about forty feet up in the canopy. It darts out after a passing insect, wings and tail spread, then turns in mid-air and flies back to disappear in the treetop. Already, this behavior has given you a clue. Perhaps the bird is some kind of flycatcher. From the direction of the unknown flycatcher, your ears pick up a loud, rolling "*wheep*" or "*preet*" issuing from across the stream. However, since you are unfamiliar with the call, why not continue to wait for the bird to reappear?

Again, the flycatcher's floppy flight succeeds in nabbing an insect on the wing. You note a flash of reddish brown in the wings and tail, and some yellow on the belly. This time, however, the bird returns to a more exposed post in the tree. You can get him in your binoculars at last, as he struggles to gulp down his latest meal. The silhouette checks out for a member of the flycatcher family. The bird sits up straight, with a medium-length floppy tail. This species is smaller than a robin, but much larger than the tiny *Empidonax* flycatchers you have been reading about. The bird has a bushy crest he can raise or lower, an olive head, gray chest, yellow belly and a rufous tail. Looking at the head, you see a strong, slender slightly flat bill, perfect for an insect diet. This is a Great Crested Flycatcher. His loud, throaty whistles echo about the treetops from early May on, for he has just arrived here to nest from wintering in Central America. The "flycatcher behavior" you observed was a helpful clue, the overall shape was that of a medium-sized flycatcher and your checklist shows the Great Crested is common in woods from May to September. These flycatchers nest high up in tree cavities;

Black-capped Chickadee

Great Crested Flycatcher

they have a legendary fondness for lining their nests with a piece of discarded snake skin, but these days it is more likely to be a piece of plastic wrap or aluminum foil. Evidently, they like something shiny in the nest.

Retracing the pathway, you head towards the exit. Right now all you want to do is go home, pour yourself a cup of coffee, and sit down to study the field guide in order to make sure your first bird identifications are correct. You cannot resist pausing, however, when one last bird catches your attention. You raise the binoculars. This is a little mite of a bird, the smallest you have seen all morning. It is much smaller than a House Sparrow. Its plump-bodied, long-tailed look and delicate bill remind you of a titmouse, but it has no crest. Alighting upside down on the underside of leaves and twigs, this little bird proceeds to glean insects while hanging there. It gives a plaintive *"fee-bee."* The plumage gives the bird away. The white cheeks that separate the black cap from the black bib below are indicative of a Black-capped Chickade. You note the white breast, gray back and buffy sides. Black-caps are resident here year-round, according to your checklist.

Chickadees are probably familiar to even the casual observer. Their friendliness around backyard feeders in winter endears them to many people. You remember that their traditional *"chick-a-dee-dee-dee"* call is accompanied in spring by a sad sounding high-pitched *"fee-bee."* In fall and winter chickadees join nuthatches, creepers and kinglets in small flocks to forage through the woodlands. They respond to pishing and to owl imitations, becoming easily agitated.

Retiring home, you will want to start a notebook with the species you identified on this walk and short descriptions of their behaviors and habitats. Here are the birds you found this morning, in the order of their appearance:

Blue Jay	Downy Woodpecker
Song Sparrow	Northern Cardinal
House Wren	Yellow Warbler
Brown Thrasher	Great Crested Flycatcher
Red-eyed Vireo	Black-capped Chickadee

A WESTERN BIRDWALK

This May morning in coastal California dawns with a light layer of fog covering the land in gray overcast, obscuring the sun. Although the weather appears gloomy to start, the fog will fade to bright sun as the day progresses. You have just entered a county park lying adjacent to low foothills. Chaparral and scrub oak clothe the hillside. Down the small ravine to your left, sycamore and bay trees soften the dry landscape, lining the course of a tiny creek. As you strike off along the trail towards the creek, the number of birds and the variety of calls they are giving seem overwhelming. Your biggest dilemma is which bird to focus on first with your binoculars.

The trail leads around some large boulders and up a gentle hill. Right away, you spot two medium-sized brown birds hopping about at the base of a bush. They seem almost trustingly tame. With your binoculars, you examine them closely. Looking at the head first, you note the conical bill. Could it be a sparrow or a finch? The bird is using its feet to disturb grubs amongst the dead leaves by scratching back and forth. This ground feeding behavior points to a kind of sparrow, but it seems too large for a typical one. However, if you have done your homework, you will remember that a towhee is a large sparrow. But what species of towhee is this? Checking for field marks, you are forced to come up with the following: a non-descript brown bird with a longish tail. But, that is all the information you need. The regional checklist shows only two kinds of towhees here. This bird is obviously not the colorful Rufous-sided Towhee. This plain brown denizen of chaparral and oak woodland is a Brown Towhee. Perhaps no other bird is as visible in California gardens and parks on the coastal plain. Brown Towhees are year-round residents. When startled, they fly jerkily, spreading their wings and tail to the full just before landing in a wood pile or shrub.

Brown Towhee

Remember how helpful it is to study the bird's overall shape and size, before getting stuck on plumage details. In this case, the bird's manner of feeding was a key behavioral clue as well.

The trail continues its leisurely climb over a small rise. Nearby, a clump of ancient live oaks seems a promising place to pause. Suddenly here comes a woodpecker, swooping up and down in flight as it approaches the largest oak tree. You glimpse the woodpecker's white rump and the broad white patches on the wings as it flies. Upon landing on a gnarled branch of the oak, the bird utters a loud, grating *"chak-a, chak-a, chak-a"* dying off at the end. It is greeted by two other similar looking woodpeckers who remain preoccupied in their search of the tree trunk. Through the binoculars you can see the entire trunk of this old oak is riddled with holes, most of which contain a single acorn. There are literally hundreds and hundreds of acorns stored there.

As the woodpecker searches the bark for an empty hole to stash its acorn, you observe its head carefully. The pattern shows a white forehead and cheeks, and crimson cap. A good rule with woodpeckers is: males always exhibit more red on their heads than females. Most female woodpeckers have no red; but when they do, it is a smaller patch. This is an Acorn Woodpecker, and both males and females have red on their heads. Female Acorn Woodpeckers have a black band separating the forehead from the crown, thus diminishing the red.

Acorn Woodpeckers are abundant in their range, which is restricted to California and the southwest. Their large white wing patches are a key field mark in flight. Their harsh, grating call, often heard from telephone poles in suburban areas, is unmistakable.

Acorn Woodpecker

Engrossed in the woodpecker, you fail to notice another bird in the huge oak. This one is now visible as it works its way down the main trunk, head first, foraging around one side of the trunk and then the other.

Shortly, it flies up to a thick limb of the tree, where it is joined by a female, resembling the male. Focus your binoculars on this chunky bird as it works the tree trunks like a woodpecker going the wrong way. There is only one group of birds that exhibits this behavior: the nuthatches. See that little, chisel-like bill? And the thick body with the blunt tail? This is a nuthatch silhouette. The bird's call is a sharp, nasal *"keer, keer"* as it travels along the oak limb.

From the checklist, you know the White-breasted Nuthatch is most likely to be breeding here in the lowlands. But you make sure by checking the bird's field marks for plumage characteristics. This bird is bluish gray with a black cap, white face and white breast. The Red-breasted Nuthatch, another species, would have had a black line through the eye with a white eyebrow above it. The Pygmy Nuthatch, another possibility, is eliminated because it has a gray-brown cap reaching to the eye. Therefore, you have successfully named one more new bird for the morning. Congratulations!

Bushtit

White-breasted Nuthatch

In spite of your intentions, it is impossible to leave this clump of oaks. Birds have been flying in and out and you have not been able to see them clearly enough to know their family, much less the species. Instead of getting frustrated, relax and take your time. Often birds will congregate in certain areas if the food supply is plentiful, and other birds will be drawn there to investigate. You can benefit by remaining perfectly still and watching all the activity around you as the presence of several birds attracts still more.

Looking up as you stand beneath the spreading oak, you now spot a curious object, so blended with the tree itself you would never have noticed it, had a tiny bird not flown directly to it and disappeared within. It is a bulky, elongated pouch made of lichens and moss hanging from the outer branches. This must be a bird's nest. Looking somewhat like a dirty sock, the pendulous structure has a hole in the side at the top. Your binoculars assist you in seeing a very small bird as it leaves the nest and flies twittering off to a near bush. The bird is plump-bodied and long-tailed, its overall size is much smaller than a House Sparrow. The bill and shape are reminiscent of a chickadee, but the tail is proportionately longer. The bird is so tiny, and its coloring so plain that it's camouflaged completely in the chaparral vegetation. Gray above and paler below with a brown crown, this midget of a bird is a Bushtit. It constructs a long, grayish nest in oaks and travels in pairs only in the breeding season. The remainder of the year, Bushtits join other family groups to form flocks, like the chickadees in the East. Watch these flocks as they pass from bush to tree, communicating with each other through a special high twitter. This sound will become even more high-pitched and sustained if a hawk should fly over. Bushtit flocks are famous for attracting other birds which travel along with them. Warblers, even some unusual ones, have been known to associate with Bushtits, so check out every bird in the flock during your fall birdwalks.

At last, you decide to resume hiking the trail. The sun is slowly peeking through the clouds, but the morning remains chilly. From the brush covered hillside a raucous "*tschek tschek*" warns the world you are approaching. A long-tailed bird with blue wings comes flying down to the path and alights. "*Ker-wheek?*" it queries harshly as it bobs its head in indignation at your intrusion into its territory. This silhouette with a strong bill and a long tail hanging straight down, belongs to a Scrub Jay. Perching atop the nearest shrub, he again questions the goings on of nature, "*ker-wheek?*" in a rasping voice.

This jay lacks a crest and is a common inhabitant of the scrub oak and chaparral community. Another western jay, the

Steller's, is closely related to the eastern Blue Jay and, like it, possesses a crest. However, in California the Steller's Jay is found at higher elevations and in more moist surroundings.

Notice the Scrub Jay's manner of flying. Its undulating flight with wings first flapping then held stiffly in a downward glide can help pinpoint it from a distance. On previous birdwalks, we have observed Scrub Jays plucking nestlings from other birds' nests while the parents fluttered helplessly about in distress.

Red-tailed Hawk

Scrub Jay

Climbing on up the hill, you reach the top and stop to rest. A sandstone boulder, now warmed by the emerging sun, beckons as a place to scan the sky above for raptors. In mid-morning the thermal air currents assist hawks as they soar high up in search of prey. A black speck, seen in the distance circling over a low ridge, materializes as an unknown hawk when viewed through the binoculars. Quickly, you rule out a possible Turkey Vulture; the wings are not tilted upwards slightly in flight and the bird does not rock from side to side. It soars on broad wings using its wide, fan-shaped tail as a rudder. What would be a good guess from this silhouette? A buteo hawk. The steady flight and wide wings held horizontally give you important clues. Now all you need to figure out is which buteo you have.

As the hawk sails lazily closer and closer, look for plumage details that translate into field marks. The tail is certainly a distinct reddish brown. You can even see the dark shoulder patches that form a bar on the leading edge of the wing. Both these are clues to a Red-tailed Hawk. Also, there is a dark belly band of streaks against whitish underparts, as you look from below. The widespread and common Red-tailed Hawk can be seen no matter what section of the country you bird. Learn to recognize it anywhere.

All of a sudden, a high-pitched squealing rips through the peaceful morning. It must be coming from the Red-tail. It is. And again, a single fierce scream echoes through the chaparral.

Looking up, you witness a scene of classic harassment. The Red-tailed Hawk is being "bombed" and dived at by another, smaller bird. The smaller bird flies rapidly with long narrow wings, slightly bent at the "wrist." Time after time, this bird appears to swoop down and attack the Red-tail. The latter, although annoyed, remains unhurried in its course, and soars over the hill and out of sight. Meanwhile, the little fellow, evidently satisfied the threat to his territory has been averted, flies swiftly over to a tall sycamore snag and lands there.

From the shape of the bird in flight, and its manner of flying rapidly with narrow wings, you have already guessed correctly it might be some kind of falcon. Focusing in on the perched bird's head, you see the hooked beak of a bird of prey. The head pattern shows two black lines, one before and one behind the eye on a white face. Moving to the rest of the body, notice the reddish-brown back and tail and the bluish-gray wing color.

What kind of falcon would be common in this area? The rare Peregrine is not a possibility, this bird is too small, anyway. Another small falcon could be a Merlin (Pigeon Hawk), but you know they breed far to the north, plus they are much darker. An American Kestrel, however, fits the description of the bird you have. Those dark "whisker" marks on the face are diagnostic. As you watch, the kestrel is joined by another, this one a bit larger. It is the female, and has no blue on the wings. In most birds of prey, the female bird is larger than the male.

The male kestrel departs to hunt above the hillside once more. You watch from a distance as he begins to hover in place, wings rapidly beating, gazing down at the unlucky grasshopper or mouse that will be his next meal. Kestrels, formerly called Sparrow Hawks, are the most common falcon through the states.

Down the hill to the creek, you follow the dusty trail towards the bottom of the shallow ravine. A few bay and

American Kestrel

sycamore trees grow here, showing the availability of scarce water in this dry land. Wait...there is a bird hopping from branch to branch in the sycamore. It is very small. Your binoculars show a flicker of olive-green as it gleans insects from the underside of the large leaves. The bird is very active, fluttering from twig to leaf.

From the head and bill shape, your first hunch that it is a wood warbler is born out. The thin, pointed bill and tiny shape are certainly warbler-like. Do you know a few of the common warblers of the western states? Compared to eastern woodlands, western habitats support remarkably few warblers. The common breeders are easily memorized: Nashville Warbler, MacGillivray's Warbler, Black-throated Gray Warbler, Yellow Warbler, Wilson's Warbler, Yellow-rumped Warbler, Orange-crowned Warbler and Common Yellowthroat.

Scanning for plumage details you notice the following: olive-green above, paler below, faint yellowish eyeline, no wing bars. The bird is so drab, and yet this description is just what you need. It fits an Orange-crowned Warbler exactly. The actual orange crown is seldom seen in the field. Orange-crowneds breed throughout the west in open woodlands, forest edges and thickets. This warbler utters a sharp metallic "*tsip*," its standard chip. In early spring, it has a wonderful crescendo of a trill, a soothing song and an important one to learn if you birdwatch in the West.

Orange-crowned Warbler

At last you have come upon the tiny trickle of water that masquerades as a creek. Small pools punctuate the water's course. Perching on one of the low boulders by the creek's shallow bank is a curious bird. Your first impression is of a tail flared and pumped, as it sits on the rock. Then, this small bird, about the size of a House Sparrow, darts off the rock in pursuit of a passing insect; you can even hear the click of the bill in mid-air as he captures his snack. This behavior certainly indicates some kind of flycatcher. The bird's plumage gives an overall impression of black and white.

As the flycatcher rests, this time on a protruding low twig, you are given time to focus your binoculars on the bird. Beginning with the head, you note the slender, flat bill. Next you remark on the black upperparts contrasting with the pure white areas of the belly coming together in a vested or "V" shape. It looks like a miniature cutaway coat, and gives this flycatcher a special, snappy costume.

If you have familiarized yourself with western flycatchers, you will know there are generally four categories: the very tiny *Empidonax* flycatchers (Western Flycatcher), the phoebes (Say's and Black), the pewees (Western Wood-Pewee) and the big flycatchers (Western Kingbird, Ash-throated Flycatcher). The phoebes are the least shy and the easiest to identify. The others are more retiring and present plumage differences that are more subtle.

The Black Phoebe is the flycatcher you have spotted at the creek. He is conspicuous, rather friendly, and prefers habitats near water where he constructs a nest largely of mud under a bridge or on a ledge. The typical flycatcher tail-pumping action gave you a hint of the bird's family even before you witnessed his characteristic manner of obtaining food. This phoebe is distinguished from a Say's by its definitive black and white plumage pattern.

Black Phoebe

In scrutinizing the Black Phoebe, your gaze has picked up a flurry of splashing and bathing in the background, caused by some dusky-streaked birds, a few of which have a brick red head, throat and breast. Here is another birdwatching puzzle. What can you deduce from looking at their silhouette? Studying the head first, you notice the conical bill, somewhat like a canary. It is either a finch, or perhaps a sparrow. You watch the birds a bit longer. Two of them fly down from the upper branches of the sycamore and join the bathing group. Others, after preening by the stream, fly off swiftly, chattering to each other in cheery tones. They could be sparrows, but they are relatively short tailed and they are not staying on the ground for long. Their flight is strong, accented by calls among themselves. These qualities point to a finch rather than a sparrow.

Within the finch family, the male House, Purple and Cassin's Finches all have reddish heads, breasts and rumps. The females are covered with dusky brown streakings. However, the House Finch is the most abundant, found in gardens, farmlands and open habitats. If you learn to recognize the House Finch, you will be able to identify 95% of the birds that come to western backyard feeders. These good natured little finches, sometimes called linnets, are fond of human environments. Often they are the first bird you will notice when you get started in birding in the West. In the East, where they were introduced forty years ago, House Finches are less common, but increasing in numbers.

Plumage variations between House, Purple and Cassin's Finches take some extra time and practice, particularly in differentiating between the streaky brown females. Learning the House Finch's field marks thoroughly will hasten your progress.

House Finch

Having spent a couple of hours on your walk, you now return to the car to head home. Be sure to check over your field guide to study the birds you have seen today. And your notebook should have important information you have jotted down about various species. You successfully spotted the following birds, definitely a good beginning:

Brown Towhee
Acorn Woodpecker
White-breasted Nuthatch
Bushtit
Scrub Jay
Red-tailed Hawk
American Kestrel
Orange-crowned Warbler
Black Phoebe
House Finch

After reading these two sample birdwalks, you can probably understand for the first time how crucial it is to know bird distribution. If you understand from a checklist what birds breed or winter in your locality, you can reduce the possibilities to only those species relevant to your region. It is unlikely you will come upon a rare bird that does not belong in your part of the country on these first birdwalks. Learning and appreciating the common birds is the best foundation a beginning birder can have.

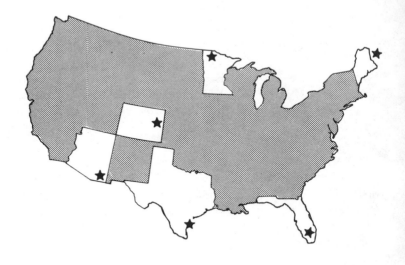

6. Birding Hot Spots

There are many kinds of field trips. As a beginner you will probably want to study areas close to your home first. After you have explored the local parks and the most interesting corners of your county, you may want to visit parts of the country that are totally unfamiliar. In this chapter we have spotlighted six unique areas in the United States noted for their spectacular birdlife. Due to the geographical locations and the habitats thus created, the bird populations found there are unusually interesting. The six hot spots are: eastern Colorado, coastal Texas, southern Florida, northeastern Minnesota, southeastern Arizona and the northeast coast of Maine along with the Gaspé Peninsula. Each of these localities is famous for diverse reasons. Many can be visited on the organized bird tours advertised in birding magazines, or you can travel there on your own. This chapter will discuss briefly what specialties are in store for you at each spot.

EASTERN COLORADO

Visiting Colorado you can see where two of North America's great faunal regions come together: the Rocky Mountains and the Great Plains. To the east, stretch the wide prairies of the Great Plains, where eastern birds are common. To the west, the Rockies rise in rugged peaks exceeding 14,000 feet, and here nearly all the birds are western species.

Within the state are significant elevational changes, and different birds are found at different altitudes, corresponding to the plant communities thriving there. The White-tailed Ptarmigan, which breeds in the Alpine-Arctic tundra above timberline, is one of the reasons to visit Colorado. Other species of interest to birdwatchers include the Rosy Finch, Williamson's Sapsucker, Hammond's and Dusky Flycatchers, Mountain Bluebird, Pine Grosbeak, Cassin's Finch and the rare Black Swift. Special birds avidly sought on the plains include the Swainson's and Ferruginous Hawks, Mountain Plover, Lark Bunting, Brewer's Sparrow, McCown's and Chestnut-collared Longspur.

The following plant zones are encountered, travelling from a point east of Denver and ending atop the high peaks of the Rockies.

Upper Sonoran

Elevation 3,500 to 6,000 feet. The average rainfall here is thirteen inches and the principal plants are grasses, yucca, cacti and Plains Cottonwood. Most of the grasslands in Colorado are short grass prairie. Grasslands are created when the rainfall is not sufficient for a forest, but abundant enough to prevent more arid conditions. Lying in the rain shadow of the Rocky Mountains, the grasses here grow five to six inches high. At preserves such as Comanche National Grassland and Pawnee National Grassland, you may get a chance to view the rare Greater and Lesser Prairie-Chickens if you visit between March and May when they are on their strutting grounds. Mountain Plover, Horned Larks, and McCown's and Chestnut-collared Longspurs also breed here in the short buffalo-grass prairie.

Transition Zone

Elevation 6,000 to 8,000 feet. Here the average rainfall is sixteen inches annually, and the chief vegetation consists of Ponderosa Pine, Narrow-leafed Cottonwood, Gambel's Oak, Douglas Fir and Blue Spruce.

Species breeding here include:

> Band-tailed Pigeon
> Broad-tailed Hummingbird
> Williamson's Sapsucker
> Dusky Flycatcher
> Pygmy Nuthatch
> Solitary Vireo
> Warbling Vireo
> Ovenbird
> Yellow Warbler

Canadian Zone

Elevation 8,000 to 10,000 feet. Average rainfall is up to twenty-seven inches annually. Vegetation includes Engelmann's Spruce, Subalpine Fir, Limber Pine, and Bristlecone Pine. This area of the higher mountains includes Rocky Mountain National Park with its famous Trail Ridge Road which leads you to spectacular scenery and many unusual birds.

Species breeding here include:

> Northern Goshawk
> Blue Grouse
> Hammond's Flycatcher
> Olive-sided Flycatcher
> Gray Jay
> Red-breasted Nuthatch
> Hermit Thrush
> Swainson's Thrush
> Townsend's Solitaire
> Wilson's Warbler
> Cassin's Finch
> Pine Grosbeak
> Red Crossbill

Among birds nesting more widely on the forest slopes are:
>Northern Three-toed Woodpecker
>Violet-green Swallow
>Tree Swallow
>Steller's Jay
>Clark's Nutcracker
>Mountain Chickadee
>Yellow-rumped Warbler
>MacGillivray's Warbler
>Pine Siskin

Alpine-Arctic

Above 11,500 feet. This section, above timberline, is known as alpine tundra. The tundra grows in extremes of cold, caused by high altitude. Many plants grow in thick mats or plump cushions, hugging the ground for protection against the snow and wind. The White-tailed Ptarmigan is well-suited for this habitat; unlike other grouse, it develops feathers on its toes in winter. These feathers are used for warmth and camouflage, and give the birds' feet extra purchase on the snow, rather like snowshoes. In sub-zero temperatures, ptarmigans dig long burrows in the snow to find twigs and leafbuds for food. Only the ptarmigan, the Rosy Finch and the Water Pipit breed at this altitude.

White-tailed Ptarmigan

The summer months are the best time to visit Colorado with its breath-taking scenery and wealth of life zones. The wildflowers are at their peak then, and many birds are nesting. Also, the higher mountain roads are all accessible by the end of June. Birds of the prairies and lower elevations nest earlier. To see the grouse and prairie-chickens, you should visit in March, April or May when the birds are actively booming.

Plain Chachalaca

COASTAL TEXAS

With nearly 550 species recorded within its borders, the huge state of Texas is extraordinarily rich in birds. It is so large that both western and eastern species reside there, depending upon which part of the state you visit.

Extending for 380 miles between Louisiana and Mexico, the Texas coast has a shoreline of barrier sand beaches teeming with shorebirds and waterbirds. In springtime, large concentrations of migrant land birds pour through the coastal plain, on their way north to Canada. The extreme southern tip of the Texas coast hosts birds that are normally found in Mexico; here they have pushed their northern range limits into the nearby Lower Rio Grande Valley. The birdwatcher can see such exotic and unique species as the Plain Chachalaca, Great Kiskadee, Green Jay and Olive Sparrow.

You have three exciting reasons to visit the Texas coast with your binoculars: the myriad of breeding water birds, a concentration of migrants in April and early May, and the presence of unique Mexican species.

The Texas coast is a large flat plain; its outer shoreline is a string of long narrow islands running parallel to the mainland. At the mouths of the major rivers, shallow lagoons form with bays. These lagoons are bordered by salt marshes extending inland, blending with the grasslands of the coastal prairies. These coastal estuaries of mud flats and tidal marshes form a fluctuating environment that is sometimes wet, sometimes dry. The water ebbing through can be either salt, fresh, or a mixture of the two. This blending of salt and freshwater makes the estuaries up to thirty times more fertile than the open sea. They form a nutrient trap for many forms of tidal life, including the birds.

The Texas coast can be divided into three areas, all of which make interesting birding. The upper coast extends from the Sabine River to Port O'Connor. Here the heavy rainfall and high humidity encourage the production of rice, and huge sections of spartina-grass salt marsh abound. At Anahuac National Wildlife Refuge you can take a famous spring tour, dubbed the "rail-buggy ride," to observe the Black and Yellow Rails.

From the Corpus Christi area north, you can witness an incredible concentration of migrant birds in April or early in May, if the weather cooperates. Land birds wintering in Central America normally pass over the Texas coast relatively unseen because the prevailing southeast winds carry them inland some distance before the birds land. However, if a cold front or "norther" occurs, the wind shifts to the north and it may start to rain. This will temporarily halt migration. The exhausted birds, having just traversed the Gulf of Mexico in their long flight, will land at the nearest available spot, perhaps on High or Padre Island. If you are lucky enough to be birding at this time, you can observe cuckoos, flycatchers, orioles, tanagers, twenty or more species of warblers and other passerines literally dripping from the trees in unprecedented numbers!

The central coast of Texas from Port O'Connor to Baffin Bay is a transition zone. Inland, are mostly grasslands and some scattered scrub oak. Eastern birds reach the southwestern limits of their range here. At the Aransas Refuge near Rockport, you will have a chance to watch the only wintering population of majestic Whooping Cranes, which arrive in October and stay until April.

The lower coast from Baffin Bay south is more arid. You begin to find western species here, plus the Mexican rarities which reach their northern limits here at the southern tip of Texas. Visit the Santa Ana Wildlife Reguge or Bentsen State Park to view these exotic species.

A partial list of Texas specialties includes:

> Least Grebe
> Olivaceous Cormorant
> Anhinga
> Little Blue Heron
> Reddish Egret
> Tricolored Heron
> Yellow-crowned Night-Heron

On the east coast of Florida, salt marshes fringe the lagoons and river mouths. Glassworts, switch grasses and sharp-pointed rushes constitute the principal vegetation. On the west coast, rushes predominate, and mangroves grow in scattered clumps. Bird species include the Brown Pelican, Black Rail, Boat-tailed Grackle and Gray Kingbird.

Interior Florida, characterized by a low plain of sand and clay, contains the pinelands where the Red-cockaded Woodpecker, Brown-headed Nuthatch, Pine Warbler and Bachman's Sparrow are found. The prairies, open flat areas studded with palmettos and scrub oaks and covered with grass, are home to the Crested Caracara, Sandhill Crane, Burrowing Owl and Grasshopper Sparrow.

Florida scrublands are large tracts of sandy soil, supporting pines and oaks. The Scrub Jay is the specialized inhabitant here.

The Everglades, one of the most famous of all wildlife habitats, is a giant freshwater marsh, the southern part of which makes up Everglades National Park. Here, island-like wooded tracts called hummocks are high enough above their surroundings to support some dry soil. A lush flora of orchids, ferns and West Indian trees grows profusely. Be sure to walk the famous Anhinga Trail in Everglades National Park. Among species found in the park are: Wood Stork, White Ibis, Roseate Spoonbill, American Swallow-tailed Kite, Snail Kite, Short-tailed Hawk, Limpkin, Marbled Godwit, Long-billed Curlew, Royal Tern, Elegant Tern, Sandwich Tern, Black Skimmer, Pileated Woodpecker, Mangrove Cuckoo, Smooth-billed Ani, Black-whiskered Vireo, Prairie Warbler, and Seaside Sparrow.

Any birder visiting Florida will not want to miss the swamps. Swamps are defined as freshwater wetlands, distinguishing them from coastal wetlands. Stands of magnificent bald cypress and other hardwoods form a lush tangle of growth in the swamps. A dense crowd of epiphytic plants contribute to this subtropical forest. At Corkscrew Swamp Sanctuary, look for large nesting colonies of Wood Stork, Great Blue Heron, Great Egret, Little Blue Heron and White Ibis. Also, the Limpkin, White-crowned Pigeon, Mangrove Cuckoo, Black-whiskered Vireo and Prairie Warbler can be found.

The Florida Keys, a chain of small low-lying islands that string for 100 miles south and west off the tip of the peninsula, are breeding places for a number of the species mentioned above, plus the Great "White" Heron, a color phase of the Great Blue Heron.

In the Gulf of Mexico, seventy miles west of Key West, lie the Dry Tortugas, a fascinating archipelago that can be reached by boat or seaplane. On these barren little islands, you can see huge nesting colonies of Sooty Terns and Brown Noddies. Magnificent Frigatebirds are abundant. If you are lucky you could see a White-tailed Tropicbird, Masked Booby or Black Noddy. The islands are excellent for observing migrant land birds.

Florida, with its swamps and marshes, pinelands and prairies, is replete with unusual species for the birdwatcher to discover. It is unfortunate that habitat destruction in this century has limited the birds to restricted areas. The best time to visit Florida is late April and early May, to coincide with spring migration when local populations are augmented by migrants from the south.

NORTHEASTERN MINNESOTA

One of the greatest continuous areas of dense forest in the world is the huge northern belt of coniferous trees, called the boreal forest, which runs across North America from New England through Canada to the Pacific. This boreal forest with its accompanying bogs and lakes, is home to many highly-sought birds. If you want to see birds of the northern woods in full song and high breeding plumage, visit northeastern Minnesota in June. A few of the specialties you might encounter are:

Black-backed Woodpecker

Northern Goshawk
Spruce Grouse
Ruffed Grouse
Sharp-tailed Grouse (in grassland)
Yellow Rail (marshes)
Great Gray Owl (rare)
Boreal Owl (rare)
Northern Saw-whet Owl

Black-backed Woodpecker
Three-toed Woodpecker (rare)
Least Flycatcher
Alder Flycatcher
Yellow-bellied Flycatcher
Le Conte's Sparrow
Red Crossbill
White-winged Crossbill*

*Eighteen species of breeding warblers (including the Connecticut and Mourning) can also be found here.

The state of Minnesota has three bio-geographical sections including the northern coniferous forest in the northeast, open prairie along the western boundary, and deciduous forest in between. The coniferous forest is relatively undisturbed with stands of White Pine, Red Pine, Jack Pine, White Spruce and Balsam-fir.

Coniferous forests are usually cold, snowy areas, but they have no permafrost, as in the tundra regions. Otherwise the trees would be unable to survive. Unlike other trees, conifers do not shed their leaves at once, but do so gradually, thus earning their name of "evergreen." They have waxy, needle-shaped leaves for protection against the cold.

When spring arrives, the frozen waters of the northern woods thaw, forming bogs, and the thick patches of vegetation at their edges attract many kinds of waterfowl. These lakes and bogs support a myriad of insects in the summer, luring the birds. Woodpeckers, working their way up and down the larvae-infested bark, tap and probe for woodboring beetles. Pine siskins, grosbeaks and waxwings feed on the glut of wood insects in the spring and summer forests; normally they would feed on berries and seeds.

At the end of autumn, the lakes grow quiet, covered with a layer of ice. The waterfowl and delicate warblers fly south, while year-round residents turn to plant material for food. Waxwings return to eating berries, as do the wintering finches. Even the woodpeckers will now take seeds. The crossbills can always extract seeds from the depths of pine cones. However, in years of poor cone crops, they will fly south to other coniferous areas. Ground birds of the coniferous forest, such as the Spruce Grouse, dine on a wide variety of buds, reeds, berries and insects.

Scattered throughout Minnesota are over 15,000 lakes. No wonder it is host to thousands of waterbirds and waterfowl. The state itself gives rise to three great drainage systems: the Mississippi, the St. Louis and the Red Rivers. Along the rivers and lakes, the emergent bulrushes, cattails, sedges and duck-weeds provide ideal conditions for breeding birds such as the Pied-billed Grebe, American Bittern, Virginia Rail, Sora, Black Tern, Yellow-headed Blackbird and Swamp Sparrow.

In fall and spring, large numbers of waterfowl, passerines and shorebirds migrate through Minnesota, following the Mississippi and the Red River routes. Also, in fall, you can witness an astonishing display of hawks and other land birds migrating around the western end of Lake Superior, near the city of Duluth. From a bluff above the city, numerous raptors can be observed streaming southward.

During severe winters in the coniferous forests, birds that normally remain further north in Canada can be driven south into Minnesota. Regular visitants at this season are: Rough-legged Hawk, Northern Shrike, Bohemian Waxwing, Common Redpoll, Red Crossbill, White-winged Crossbill, Lapland Long-spur, and Snow Bunting. Occasionally, food shortages farther north will force irruptions of a particular species into northern-most Minnesota. At such times, you could see a Snowy Owl, Northern Hawk-Owl, Great Gray Owl or Boreal Owl, with luck!

SOUTHEASTERN ARIZONA

You cannot take up birdwatching for very long without hearing about southeast Arizona and its legendary birdlife and scenery. On a visit to Arizona, you can see the birds of the low Sonoran Desert and also explore several small mountain ranges famous for their rugged beauty and exotic bird species. These ranges—the Santa Rita, the Huachuca and the Chiri-cahua among them—rise like ecological islands from the surrounding desert floor to a height of over 9,000 feet. The mountains lure many Mexican species because they form the northern terminus of the Sierra Madre Mountains of Mexico. Thus, in this remote corner of Arizona, there are twenty-five species of birds typically found nowhere else in the United States. Another thirty are found only here, in Texas or New Mexico. Such species as Montezuma Quail, Blue-throated and Magnificent Hummingbirds, Elegant Trogon, Bridled Titmouse, Sulphur-bellied Flycatcher, Red-faced Warbler and Painted Redstart make the birding superb.

If you have never birded the southwestern desert, studded with giant saguaro cacti and alive with unique desert birds, be sure to do so before you climb into the mountains. In the desert the landscape may appear dead, but it is simply lying dormant until the rains come, when it will pulsate with a pageant of plants and birds in renewed activity. The fantastic species of cacti, with their thick, rounded bodies built to slow down evaporation, have no leaves but are armed with deadly spikes and thorns. They trap energy in their fat stems and have wide, shallow root systems. The Giant Saguaro Cactus, which grows to a height of fifty feet and can live for 200 years, consists almost entirely of stored water. Here the "Gilded" Flicker and Gila Woodpecker excavate their holes, later to be reused by American Kestrels, Elf Owls, Western Screech-Owls, Brown-crested Flycatchers and Purple Martins. Other birds, such as the White-winged Doves, eat the bright, red fruits that follow the saguaro's waxy blossoms. These strange cacti are pollinated by long-tongued bats which hover in front of the flowers and sip the nectar.

In the low desert, birds forage at dawn and dusk to avoid extreme midday heat. The numerous insect-eating birds gain moisture from their prey. Desert birds court, nest and finish breeding quickly, taking advantage of the brief rainy periods. They have adapted themselves wonderfully to this stark environment. For example, the Gambel's Quail does not even attempt to pair unless rainfall has produced sufficient vegetation for a plentiful food supply. The Common Poorwill "sleeps" in crevices in rocks during the cold, dry winter and only comes out of its torpor when insect food is abundant. Many birds depart the desert in the dry season.

Other plants making up the typical desert landscape include creosote bush, mesquite, brittle bush, cholla and prickly pear. The Sonoran desert is home to the Cactus Wren, Verdin, various thrashers, Black-tailed Gnatcatcher and Black-throated Sparrow.

The mountain ranges of southeastern Arizona are covered with Evergreen Oak, Manzanita, Juniper and Pinyon Pine on the lower slopes. Towards the summits, conifers such as Ponderosa Pine and Douglas Fir form tall stands, and it is hard to realize the desert floor is little over an hour away by car. In the Huachuca Mountains, be sure to visit Ramsay Canyon, where more than a dozen species of hummingbirds have been spotted at feeders. In the Chiricahua range you can locate the gorgeous Elegant Trogon, and then climb to the high forests to see Grace's and Olive Warblers, Yellow-eyed Juncos and Mexican Chickadees.

Arizona's climate is one of almost constant sunshine. Midsummer temperatures around Tucson are over 100 degrees in the day. However, the mountain ranges are considerably more temperate. The time to visit Arizona varies depending upon your priorities. To see most of the standard breeding birds, come in late May through June. However, the summer rains make July and August quite pleasant in Arizona. This is the time when additional Mexican rarities often wander north.

A brief list of Arizona specialties includes:

Elegant Trogon

Black-bellied Whistling-Duck
Mississippi Kite
Zone-tailed Hawk
Gray Hawk
Common Black-Hawk
Scaled Quail
Montezuma Quail
Magnificent Hummingbird
Berylline Hummingbird
Blue-throated Hummingbird

Violet-crowned Hummingbird
White-eared Hummingbird
Elegant Trogon
Strickland's Woodpecker
Rose-throated Becard
Tropical Kingbird
Thick-billed Kingbird
Sulphur-bellied Flycatcher
Buff-breasted Flycatcher
Vermilion Flycatcher
Northern Beardless-Tyrannulet
Greater Pewee
Gray-breasted Jay
Mexican Chickadee
Bridled Titmouse
Bendire's Thrasher
Virginia's Warbler
Lucy's Warbler
Olive Warbler
Grace's Warbler
Red-faced Warbler
Painted Redstart
Hepatic Tanager
Varied Bunting
Abert's Towhee
Yellow-eyed Junco

NORTHEAST COAST OF MAINE & GASPÉ PENINSULA

Any account of birdwatching spots would be incomplete without a mention of the spectacle of thousands of nesting seabirds on the islands off the coast of Maine and further north around Bonaventure Island off the Gaspé Peninsula in Quebec. Between mid-May and August, you can procure a boat to take you around these rocky islands where Northern Gannets, Black Guillemots, Black-legged Kittiwakes, Common Murres, Razorbills, Herring Gulls and Atlantic Puffins nest in huge colonies.

A tiny island, Machias Seal Island, lies between Maine and New Brunswick. Another, Matinicus Island, lies approximately fifteen miles from the coast of Maine and is the largest of the

Matinicus Archipelago. Both are famous oceanic bird islands, alive with Leach's Storm-Petrels, Arctic Terns, Common Terns, Razorbills, and Atlantic Puffins. Arctic Terns nest on the grassy areas of Machias Island, dive bombing any intruders. It is difficult to imagine the newly hatched juvenile terns will migrate far south of the equator to spend the winter. Razorbills and puffins hide their single eggs under the rocks. The adult puffins fish off the rocks, then carry fish in their bills to the chicks. When ready to fend for themselves, the youngsters are abandoned by the adults.

Moving north to Quebec, you can embark on a boat for Bonaventure Island. The village of Percé at the tip of the Gaspé Peninsula is the place to start your seabird tour. Thousands of Northern Gannets, Razorbills, Black Guillemots, Black-legged Kittiwakes, Common Murres and Atlantic Puffins nest on the cliffs of Bonaventure. At least 20,000 pairs of gannets nest on the island, making it one of the largest of the North American ganneries.

On the larger islands such as Bonaventure and on the mainland of the Gaspé peninsula, you will find good land birding as well. In the forests of balsam-fir and spruce, expect to find many species of breeding warblers and other passerines. Early June to early August is the best time. Visiting islands off the coast of Maine, New Brunswick and Quebec is well worth the ingenuity it may take to reach some of them. Strong tides, erratic sea conditions and foggy weather require an experienced navigator. You will have to obtain information locally about such individuals and their boats.

A partial list of sea birds breeding on northern islands:

Northern Gannet

Leach's Storm-Petrel
Northern Gannet
Double-crested Cormorant
Common Eider
Great Black-backed Gull
Herring Gull
Black-legged Kittiwake
Common Tern
Arctic Tern
Razorbill
Common Murre

Black Guillemot
Atlantic Puffin

A partial list of land birds includes:
Spruce Grouse
Ruffed Grouse
Yellow-bellied Flycatcher
Alder Flycatcher
Gray Jay
Boreal Chickadee
Winter Wren
Golden-crowned Kinglet
Ruby-crowned Kinglet
Gray-cheeked Thrush
Philadelphia Vireo
Tennessee Warbler
Northern Parula
Magnolia Warbler
Black-throated Green Warbler
Bay-breasted Warbler
Blackpoll Warbler
Black-and-white Warbler
Pine Grosbeak
Fox Sparrow
Lincoln's Sparrow

7. Birding Activities and Projects

You don't have to be a scientist to discover unknown facts about the birds around us. Amateur naturalists can make many contributions in birdwatching. Your observations and sightings can be used to piece together answers to many puzzles of bird behavior. Accurate dates of sightings can help define migratory patterns. Your counts can help confirm estimates of the size of resident populations. Careful observations help experts determine feeding ranges and nesting habits. On a personal level you should keep records of your field trips and sightings to help you learn the birds and to keep fresh the memory of your experiences. And, your records can be integrated with those of others to help scientists understand more clearly what is going on in the bird world.

If you keep your notebooks carefully and accurately, especially if you keep them over long periods of time, you may want to think about preserving them permanently in the archive section of a local natural history museum, university or library. After you have several years' worth of notes, contact some local organization and ask if they catalog and keep this kind of material. Your hobby needn't be a private recreation; sharing your information can be satisfying and it may come as a wonderful revelation to some researcher struggling along with minimal funding and only one pair of eyes.

This chapter will teach you how to keep lists and records, and will show you some interesting projects to deepen your knowledge of the birds. Keeping lists and field notes is an excellent way to learn the birds, and your enthusiasm will increase immensely as your lists get longer and longer. You needn't be an expert to conduct the backyard projects we describe here. But you will find yourself feeling like an expert when you have identified some interesting aspect of bird behavior and observed it for a while.

STARTING YOUR LISTS

Most birdwatchers keep lists. On your first few field trips you may feel you will never forget your first sightings of the notable birds of your area. However, you are going to be seeing a lot of birds as you get more involved, and memories are subject to change and subconscious editing. Hence, the necessity for listing. Many field guides provide checklists, or an area in the index where you can check off each species as you see it. Some birders prefer to annotate the field guide itself, noting the date and location of each sighting next to the printed description of the bird. Both these habits can lead to messy guides and some confusions as the limited space is used up and overlapped with new notes.

In the Appendix we have provided you with a list of birds found in North America. You can photocopy this list and use it as your basic checklist, or make notes in this book. There are many different types of lists you can keep. Perhaps the most basic is a *life* list, a record of every species of bird you spot in your birdwatching career. Some birders travel extensively and build up an enormous life list, but this requires a deep commitment of time and money, and may not match your interests at all. Another kind of list is the *year* list. You start a new year list every January and see how many birds you total for that year. These lists, of course, are more interesting when you compare several years at a time. Many birders keep *state* and *county* lists as well. The kind of list that should appeal to most beginners is the *locale* or *trip* list. Here you record every species you locate in either a specific locale, or on a given trip. A final list that might interest you would be a *season* list of birds sighted during a specific time span, (*e.g.*, fall or spring).

Comparing lists leads to interesting insights into the behavior of birds. Changes in year lists can reflect increased birding activities on your part, or they may reflect some large changes in the environment. Hurricanes in the Gulf Coast can blow migrating birds completely out of their familiar territories. Long droughts can change the availability of specific foods for individual birds. The damming of a river, the development of a large industrial park, or the draining of a significant wetland can dramatically change your data. Looking over season lists of birds observed in one locale can lead to some insights on migration and nesting. Some birds may move fairly quickly through your area on their way to more southerly climates or appropriate nesting grounds. If you date your sightings, these migrations can be tracked.

Checklists of the birds of North America are issued by the American Birding Association and the American Ornithologists' Union (see Appendix). More local checklists are available for specific counties or states. Check natural history museums and local birding organizations for these.

The competitive aspect of listing birds has attracted many newcomers to birding. The challenge of adding seldom seen or rare birds to one's growing list of species is undeniable. The prospect of finding the unexpected and unusual bird has led to improved coverage of many parts of the country, as birders expand their skills in field identification. However, and we really want to emphasize this point, birdwatching is much more than a lengthy list of birds you have observed! All too often, a birder may proudly point to the tabulation of several hundred species he has seen, then ticked off on a checklist, and promptly forgotten. He may not know anything about the plumage details, the geographic range or the calls of these birds. Such a birder is called, in the vernacular, a lister or a "twitcher," a word borrowed from the British. Truly experienced birdwatchers have no use for this type of activity. It is wonderful and exciting to chase rare birds, but if this is your only motivation for birdwatching, you will soon lose interest.

A true love of birds has little to do with the frequency of occurrence of the bird. Many so-called "trash" birds are just as worthy of study and attention as the rarities. Besides, it is through knowledge of the common birds that you will be able to recognize an unusual one, possibly right in your own backyard.

TAKING FIELD NOTES

Field notes contain much more information than lists. Consequently, they are more complex and detailed, and they take more time to prepare. However, the rewards more than compensate for the effort you put into your notes.

Scientists have develped a method for taking field notes that preserves much of your field experience in a systematic fashion. Our description of this method is modified from an article by J.V. Remsen in *American Birds*, September 1977. The specific field note format was developed at the Museum of Vertebrate Zoology in Berkeley by Joseph Grinnell. This format has been accepted and used by most serious bird-watchers.

The main document you keep is a journal recording each bird trip. A spiral bound notebook is fine for this purpose. All entries are made in chronological order, with the date prominently displayed. Below is a sample.

```
DATE:
AREA:                          TIME:
WEATHER:
OBSERVERS:
SPECIES    NO. OBSERVED    SPECIES    NO. OBSERVED
```

You should also keep a species notebook. In this book you would devote a separate page for each species where you note your sightings for that year. This way you can refer back and see how many times, and in which locations, you spotted each individual species. The following is a sample format for your species notebook.

```
                        SPECIES
DATE              LOCATION              NO OBSERVED
```

Along with these records, you will probably want to devote a page to describing each species in much more detail. Head up each page with the date, location, and species. Then write your observation of the bird(s). Include the behaviors you observed, details of plumage and song, and any other information that may be relevant. Don't be short on detail here, you will never duplicate this exact field trip again, and you can never anticipate what information may interest you later.

In taking notes on a field trip, try to group your information by habitat stops. For example, if you are visiting a specific valley and you see a number of birds en route, do not lump them in with the totals for the whole valley. They are separate data and should be described as such. Once you arrive at the valley, try to keep track of the birds you see at each stop. It tells us nothing if your trip list shows 150 Lesser Scaup. Where were they? Flying over? On a lake? On a reservoir en route? Where the birds were seen is just as important as the time of year and the quantity.

You will learn the birds much faster if you keep systematic notes. Later on you can look back and refresh your memory, preserving your field trips for many years. These notes will provide invaluable information on the natural history of the areas you visit. Don't be embarrassed to take notes on common birds, you needn't spot only rare or unusual species. You may not know for years what important data lies in your field notes, but the more detailed and systematic you make them, the more they can be used.

Facsimile of Jon Dunn's Notebook.

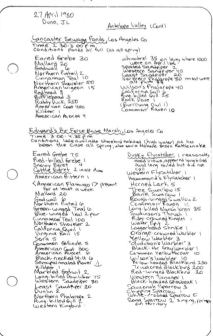

HABITAT MAPPING YOUR COMMUNITY

A habitat map is a wonderful tool for understanding the ecological dynamics of any area. Living in manmade environments with neat grid-like street arrangements we tend to forget the natural landscapes of our communities. Even in relatively small areas, a patient observer can find a surprisingly large range of different habitats. You should visit all these environments in order to view the full wealth of bird life.

To construct a habitat map, choose a logical area to study. Perhaps you will want to look at your city or county, depending on their size. Obtain a map of the site you have chosen and start hunting for the obvious landmarks. You can color them with felt tip pens according to a color-coded scheme. Look for the watery environments first because they are richest in wildlife of all kinds. The water will support the growth of many plants, insects and small animals that the birds can live on. Mark the rivers, streams, lakes and sloughs first. Don't forget such manmade sites as reservoirs, ornamental lakes, sewage sludge ponds, etc. They will attract their share of wildlife, too. You may want to distinguish between seasonal creeks and streams and those that run all year. You may also want to show which waterways freeze over in the winter. Along the California coast, Great Blue Herons will fly several miles inland to search out backyard ponds where they will eat all the ornamental goldfish carefully stocked by a proud homeowner. You probably won't want to be this detailed in your map, but make sure you find all the major watercourses and locations of standing water on your map.

How about mountains? Indicate approximate elevations of the mountains and hills on your map. Also, check rainfall levels. In this context, remember a mountain range will often block most of the rainfall from a moving storm so one side of the range is significantly moister than the other. Are there any arid areas near you? What about agricultural lands? These are often irrigated in summer and may attract many birds.

Local checklists of your county or city are often very specific in describing site locations. You can use these to help you with your habitat mapping. Also, talk to local birders. They will know interesting spots which attract birds. If you learn of a line of special trees that attract the fall leaf-hopping insects and consequently the fall warblers, add them to the map. If the city builds a new park with an artificial lake that the ducks discover, then include it on your map. Let your map reflect what you have learned as you gain experience in birdwatching.

STUDYING NESTING TERRITORIES AND MAKING NESTING CALENDARS

Mapping nesting territories is a good backyard project for beginning birdwatchers. Draw a simple schematic map of the area around a bird nest you have located. Indicate your house and other structures, trees and bushes, streets and sidewalks. Then carefully watch the birds. Mark your map wherever the nesting birds exhibit territorial behaviors. These behaviors can include singing, posturing and other aggressive attitudes. By carefully keeping track of these displays you can determine the boundaries of the bird's territory. Draw a line through the outermost display sites and you can see the nesting territory.

Once you are familiar enough with your backyard birds to spot their nesting activites and find where they construct their nests, you may want to start a nesting and breeding calendar. Birds nest and raise their young at different times of the year, depending on species and local conditions. Many species raise more than one brood. The following is a simple format you can use to construct a calendar for two different species. Add more species as you spot the activities of more birds.

	BIRD		BIRD	
	NESTING	BREEDING	NESTING	BREEDING
JAN.				
FEB.				
MAR.				
APR.				
MAY				
JUN.				
JUL.				
AUG.				
SEP.				
OCT.				
NOV.				
DEC.				

Mark the months in which you observe the appropriate behavior. You may have chosen birds with considerable overlap in their activities, or you may be surprised at how early or late in the season they nest and raise their young.

SURVEYING LOCAL POPULATIONS

Tabulating a population survey of the birds you commonly see is a very good way to learn bird identification and to enjoy the outdoors. Once you know some of the birds in your backyard or park, keep track of the number you spot. This sounds easier than it is and you will usually be making estimates rather than a perfectly accurate count. It is confusing to try to count the individual members of a flock of tiny bushtits or chickadees. Even with larger birds such as crows or shorebirds, you will find yourself estimating numbers. Learn to count the first group of birds in a large flock, then multiply that figure for the entire flock. This technique becomes easier with practice. Of course, there is always the dilemma of counting individual birds more than once. The hummingbird you spotted at your feeder an hour ago may turn up in your vegetable garden later on. Knowing bird calls will help in censusing bird species.

Despite the difficulties in making an accurate count, note your information in your field notes along with the date and time of day. Keep a systematic watch over the period of a year and you may see some surprising changes in the size of resident populations. you may also be able to accurately pinpoint the arrivals and departures of local migrating species.

WATCHING NOCTURNAL MIGRANTS

Moon watching is an old technique for studying nocturnal bird migrations, although nowadays scientists have replaced it with more technical approaches, including the use of radar. Nevertheless, you can still catalog the flight directions of birds migrating at night by viewing their silhouettes as they fly across the disc of the moon. Binoculars and a powerful scope are essential. More recently, a portable ceilometer has been developed, in which a beam of light is pointed vertically into the night sky. The birds are dimly illuminated from below, and observed with binoculars and scopes as they pass through the light beam. The components involved are inexpensive, and the lights can be operated off a car battery. The technique can obviously be used on many more nights than moon watching, because cloudy weather presents no impediment.

If you can find two or three friends who are interested in nocturnal migration, you can each take a viewing spot separated by several miles. Comparing data can help establish the size of the migration, the species involved and the direction in which they are moving.

THE CHRISTMAS BIRD COUNT

Each year the National Audubon Society sponsors an enormous winter census of birds. Hundreds of birders go out on a specific day during Christmas week and count species and individuals within a designated count circle of fifteen miles in diameter. The count is taken in every state and most Canadian provinces and is one of the most widespread ever attempted. The results are computerized and published in *American Birds*. This data provides information on the expansion or contraction of specific bird ranges, and provides insight into which species are thriving and which may become endangered.

Birders hunt over plains and marshes, beaches and mountainsides, by sleigh, on skiis and snowshoes, by automobile and commercial boat, and even by marsh buggy. Friendly rivalry exists between communities, usually those in the southern states, as they compete for the greatest number of species observed on this particular day. Areas in more northerly climates will probably end up tabulating fifteen or twenty different species on their counts, while the southwest, Florida and Texas can end up with count totals in the 200s.

Experienced birdwatchers identify the birds, but there are plenty of jobs for beginners. The Christmas Bird Count is a fascinating activity and a wonderful chance to become involved with birdwatching in your community. You will have a chance to meet the influential birders and you will gain experience in identification. Join the annual count this year; your efforts will help contribute to the single biggest data base on birds ever collected.

TAKING CLASSES AND NETWORKING

If at all possible, you should take a few classes when you first become interested in birdwatching. Hunting through the fields with an expert who thoroughly knows the local birds will give you insight into the sport. Without a teacher you may find yourself stuck with a strange bird in your binoculars, while trying to rapidly flip through a field guide, before the bird gets disgusted and decides to try another feeding site. The range of choices is so great to someone unfamiliar with basic birding, your chance of successfully identifying certain birds can be pretty low. Classes are offered through adult education, university extensions, community colleges, natural history museums and such wildlife associations as the Sierra Club and the National Audubon Society.

By taking classes you meet people with similar interests. After you know a few other beginning birders, set up local trips on your own and continue to add to your lists while learning more birdwatching skills. Too, you will find out which organizations are active in your community and who the local hotshots and experts are. In birding, there is a lot of friendly rivalry over the size of lists and the totals of birds sighted each year. However, there is also a tremendous amount of companionship and eagerness to help the amateur. The competition is never critical, as in other sports, and the more birders you meet the more information you can gather.

Birdwatchers as a species are social animals, sharing stories of their favorite birds (or their most humiliating defeats). A large part of the satisfaction with birding comes from joining this group of people. No matter where you live or travel, you will always know there are people to welcome you and to share the birdlife in a new corner of the world.

8. A Note on Ethics

It is 6:00 A.M., a group of twenty people in knee-high rubber boots is quietly sneaking along a creekbed behind a group of condominiums with binoculars glued to their eyeballs. This could be the beginning of a horror movie or a typical day of birdwatching. It could also be the beginning of several different kinds of problems. Birdwatchers like to travel where most people wouldn't think to set foot (or boot), and often at hours of the day or night that are considerably outside those of the normal working day. Their activities could look suspicious, or they could intrude on the privacy of others. And this is just one reason birders should adhere to a strict code of ethics.

Birdwatchers shouldn't disturb others with their activities. They should carefully honor private property and all the rules of public parks and recreation areas. Many times a group leader can obtain permission to bird on private or posted land, on condition the group respect the rights of the property owners. Violating these rights and laws will not only ruin your birdwatching trip, it could jeopardize further outings.

Twenty pairs of boots can thoroughly muddy a creek and tear up a lot of vegetation, or they can move carefully without damaging the habitat. The birds and other wildlife have rights too. We must make sure their world is protected, not harmed, by our presence. Never chase or repeatedly flush the birds just to get another glimpse. Don't touch them or their nests. Don't harm the plants they depend on for food and shelter. We should watch birds with respect, and with the hope others will act similarly.

Protect the habitats you visit on your field trips. This can include such obvious precautions as cleaning up your own litter and exercising extreme caution with fire. A careless range, forest or brush fire can wipe out generations of wildlife. Also, seemingly small changes to a habitat can have a large impact on the wildlife. Return boulders and fallen logs to their original positions if you search under them; don't change the normal course of waterways, no matter how small they are; never collect animal or plant specimens unless you are sure you have the appropriate permit. In order to observe nature closely and accurately, it is important to have as little impact on the environment as you can.

Many codes of ethical behavior have been developed for naturalists and birdwatchers. You may want to consult some of these in more detail. Especially useful is Gerald Durrell's volume *A Practical Guide for the Amateur Naturalist*. The American Birding Association also has a guideline to the ethics of good birding. This may be found in the *A.B.A. Checklist, Second Edition.*

APPENDIX

Bibliography

PERIODICALS

American Birds. National Audubon Society, 950 Third Ave., New York, N.Y., 10022. Relatively technical articles on bird distribution, Christmas Count census, etc.

Audubon. National Audubon Society, 950 Third Ave., New York, N.Y., 10022. Beautiful photographic magazine reflecting subjects of interest to conservationists and bird lovers.

Birding. American Birding Association, P.O. Box 4335, Austin, Texas, 78765. Aimed at the active birder who enjoys listing North American birds. Many good articles on identification in the field.

Bird Watcher's Digest. P.O. Box 110, Marietta, Ohio, 45750. Relaxed, anecdotal articles about birds and birdwatchers.

The Living Bird Quarterly. Cornell University Laboratory of Ornithology, 159 Sapsucker Woods Rd., Ithaca, N.Y., 14850. Members of the Laboratory of Ornithology receive this publication, a blend of scientific and broad-interest subjects.

Natural History. American Museum of Natural History, Central Park West & 79th., New York, N.Y., 10024. Excellent scientific articles on wide range of subjects written for the layman. Often includes birds, evolution, etc.

PROFESSIONAL JOURNALS

The Auk. Allen Press Inc., Box 368 Lawrence, Kansas, 66044. Published by the American Ornithologists' Union.

The Condor. Cooper Ornithological Society, Cornell University Laboratory of Ornithology, 159 Sapsucker Woods Rd., Ithaca, N.Y., 14850.

The Wilson Bulletin. Wilson Ornithological Society, Department of Ornithology, Royal Ontario Museum, 100 Queen's Park, Toronto, Ontario, M5S2C6.

These three publications are highly technical journals written primarily for professional ornithologists. They contain scientific papers on all aspects of birds from around the world.

BOOKS: Field Guides

Bull, John, and Farrand, John, Jr. *The Audubon Society Field Guide to North American Birds: Eastern Region.* New York: Alfred A. Knopf, 1977. AND Udvardy, Miklos D.F. *The Audubon Society Field Guide to North American Birds: Western Region.* New York: Alfred A. Knopf, 1977. Complete collection of North American birds, illustrated by photographs. Chief drawback in both books is that the birds are not organized by families, but by color and type.

Farrand, John, Jr., ed. *The Audubon Society Master Guide to Birding.* New York: Alfred A. Knopf, 1983. Three-volume guide for the more advanced birder. Organized by new A.O.U. classification, illustrated with color photos, up-to-date text written by experts.

Field Guide to the Birds of North America. Washington, D.C.: The National Geographic Society, 1983. Definitive field guide to North American birds, including accidentals, in one volume. Illustrated by artists, with latest information on plumage details.

Harrison, Colin. *A Field Guide to the Nests, Eggs and Nestlings of North American Birds.* Brattleboro, Vt.: The Stephen Greene Press., 1984. Complete information on types of nests, number and state of nestlings, incubation and nesting periods.

Holmgren, Virginia C. *SCANS Key to Birdwatching.* Portland, Ore.: Timber Press, 1983. Description of 200 North American birds organized according to size and color by pages keyed at the margins.

Peterson, Roger Tory. *A Field Guide to the Birds (East of the Rockies).* Boston: Houghton Mifflin, 1980. A revision of the classic field guide that popularized birdwatching in America.

Peterson, Roger Tory. *A Field Guide to the Birds of Texas.* Boston: Houghton Mifflin, 1960. Extremely useful and accurate for Texas and adjacent states.

Peterson, Roger Tory. *A Field Guide to Western Birds.* Boston: Houghton Mifflin, 1969. Another classic, now undergoing revision.

BOOKS: Older Field Guides

Chapman, Frank M. *Handbook of Birds of Eastern North America.* New York and London: D. Appleton & Co., 1930. Valuable observations on Eastern birds by a venerated birdwatcher.

Hoffman, Ralph. *Birds of the Pacific States.* Boston: Houghton Mifflin, 1927. Outstanding descriptions of bird song and behavior from a pioneer of birdwatching in the western states.

Pough, Richard H. *Eastern Land Birds. An Audubon Guide.* New York: Doubleday & Co., 1946. AND Pough, Richard H. *Eastern Water Birds. An Audubon Guide.* New York: Doubleday & Co., 1951.

AND Pough Richard H. *Audubon Western Bird Guide*. New York: Doubleday & Co., 1957. Classic field guides with lengthy, if old-fashioned, bird descriptions. Eckelberry's plates are charming and accurate.

BOOKS: General Reference

Austin, Oliver L. *Families of Birds*. A Golden Guide. New York: Golden Press, 1971. Compact, handy introduction to bird families over the world, briefly described with color illustrations.

Godfrey, W. Earl. *The Birds of Canada*. Ottawa: National Museums of Canada, 1966. Much more than a regional guide, describing over 500 different birds that occur in Canada, and their North American ranges. Large color plates by John Crosby; a superb reference work.

Pasquier, Roger F. *Watching Birds*. Boston: Houghton Mifflin, 1977. A fine introduction to ornithology, non-technical enough for an interested beginner.

Peterson, Roger Tory. *The Birds*. New York: Time/Life Inc. Nature Library, 1963. Well-illustrated, simple yet comprehensive coverage of birds and their habits. Perfect introduction.

Reilly, Edgar M. Jr. *The Audubon Illustrated Handbook of American Birds*. New York: McGraw-Hill, 1968. Lengthy accounts of over 850 birds known to occur north of Mexico, accompanied by black and white photos. Good basic reference.

Stokes, Donald W. *A Guide to the Behavior of Common Birds. Volume One*. Boston: Little, Brown and Company, 1979. AND Stockes, Donald W. and Stokes, Lillian Q. *A Guide to the Behavior of Common Birds. Volume Two*. Boston: Little, Brown and Company, 1979. Both volumes study behavior and social patterns, go beyond identification and encourage backyard study.

Terres, John K. *The Audubon Society Encyclopedia of North American Birds*. New York: Alfred A. Knopf, 1980. Comprehensive encyclopedia, illustrated discussions of nearly 6,000 topics, with cross references. Includes over 800 color photos and an enormous bibliography.

Thielcke, G.A. *Bird Sounds*. Ann Arbor, Michigan: University of Michigan Press, 1976. Thorough and readable treatment of how and why birds sing and communicate.

Van Tyne, J. and Berger, A.J. *Fundamentals of Ornithology*. New York: Dover Publications, 1976. Classic for students with some knowledge of ornithology. Useful synopsis of bird families of the world.

Welty, Joel Carl. *The Life of Birds*. Philadelphia: W.B. Saunders Co., 1982. The best standard ornithology text. Scholarly, but essential for the interested amateur.

BOOKS: Birdwatching and Other Projects

Bernstein, Chuck. *The Joy of Birding, A Guide to Better Birdwatching.* Santa Barbara, Ca.: Capra Press, 1984. Entertaining essays on major birdwatching topics, and descriptions of field trips (some with major birding experts) with many helpful tips.

Durrell, Gerald. *A Practical Guide for the Amateur Naturalist.* New York: Alfred A. Knopf, 1983. Beautifully illustrated, organized according to habitats, describes typical naturalists' activities and projects.

Harrison, George H. *The Backyard Bird Watcher.* New York: Simon & Schuster, 1979. How to attract, house, and feed birds in your backyard.

Heintzelman Donald S. *The Birdwatcher's Activity Book.* Harrisburg, Pa.: Stackpole Books, 1983. Further projects for birdwatchers.

Hickey, Joseph J. *A Guide to Birdwatching.* New York: Dover Publications, 1975. Reprint of 1943 edition, classic introduction to birdwatching and field ornithology.

Kress Stephen W. *The Audubon Society Handbook for Birders.* New York: Charles Scribner's Sons, 1981. Detailed discussions on latest in birdwatching, etc.

Richert, Jon E. *A Guide to North American Bird Clubs.* Elizabethtown, Ky.: Avian Publications, Inc., 1978. Comprehensive listing, including addresses and key officers, publications, field trips and meetings.

BOOKS: Bird Finding

Harrison, George H. *Roger Tory Peterson's Dozen Birding Hot Spots.* New York: Simon & Schuster, 1976. Maps and visitor information on special birding spots in United States.

Kitching, Jessie. *Birdwatcher's Guide to Wildlife Sanctuaries.* New York: Arco Publishing Co., Inc., 1976. Descriptions of 295 refuges in United States and Canada, with information on checklists.

Lane, James A. This author has written birdwatching guides to eastern Colorado, Florida, the Rio Grande Valley of Texas, southeastern Arizona, southern California and the Texas Coast. The guides are great for the traveler and offer much information on birds in each territory. All are available from L. and P. Press, Box 21604, Denver, Colorado, 80221.

Pettingill, Olin Sewall, Jr. *A Guide to Bird Finding East of the Mississippi.* New York: Oxford University Press, 1977. AND Pettingill, Olin Sewall, Jr. *A Guide to Bird Finding West of the Mississippi.* New York: Oxford University Press, 1981. Essential for the traveling birder. Habitats and locations of birds in each of the states, plus how to reach them.

Numerous other regional books exist, many are available through catalogs. Write to the American Birding Assocation for a list of regional books they carry.

CHECKLISTS

A.B.A. Checklist: Birds of Continental United States and Canada. Second edition. Austin, Texas: American Birding Association, 1982. Checklist with common and scientific names of North American birds, no descriptions.

Check-list of North American Birds. Sixth edition. Lancaster, Pa.: American Ornithologists' Union, 1983. Checklist with common and scientific names of North American birds, no descriptions.

CATALOGS

American Birding Association. P.O. Box 4335, Austin, Texas, 78765. Books, particularly local and regional, and numerous checklists.

The Audubon Workshop. 1501 Paddock Dr., Northbrook, Ill., 60062. Birdfeeders, seed, bird accessories.

Avicultural Book Co. P.O. Box 446, East Elmhurst, N.Y., 11369. Current books (many discounted), and records.

Avicultural Book Club. P.O. Box 446, East Elmhurst, N.Y. 11369. All selections discounted from publishers' editions.

Birding. Box 5-E, Amsterdam, N.Y., 12010. Discounts on binoculars, scopes and optical accessories.

Buteo Books. P.O. Box 481, Vermilion, S.D. 57069. Huge selection of new and used titles, including some out-of-print.

The Crow's Nest Bookshop. Laboratory of Ornithology, Cornell University, Sapsucker Woods, Ithaca, N.Y., 14850. Complete listing of books including latest editions, and many records.

Duncraft. Penacook, N.H., 03303. Birdfeeders, seed and birdhcuses.

List of North American Birds

(Canada and United States excluding Hawaii)

Sequence and taxonomy based on A.O.U. Check-list, Sixth Edition.

Loons *(Gaviidae)*

DATE(S)

☐ Red-throated Loon. *Gavia stellata* _____

☐ Arctic Loon. *Gavia arctica.* _____

☐ Common Loon. *Gavia immer* _____

☐ Yellow-billed Loon. *Gavia adamsii* _____

Grebes *(Podicipedidae)*

☐ Least Grebe. *Tachybaptus dominicus* _____

☐ Pied-billed Grebe. *Podilymbus podiceps* _____

☐ Horned Grebe. *Podiceps auritus* _____

☐ Red-necked Grebe. *Podiceps grisegena* _____

☐ Eared Grebe. *Podiceps nigricollis* _____

☐ Western Grebe. *Aechmophorus occidentalis* _____

Albatrosses *(Diomedeidae)*

☐ Short-tailed Albatross. *Diomedea albatrus* _____

☐ Black-footed Albatross. *Diomedea nigripes* _____

☐ Laysan Albatross. *Diomedea immutabilis* _____

☐ Black-browed Albatross. *Diomedea melanophris* _____

☐ Shy Albatross. *Diomedea cauta* _____

☐ Yellow-nosed Albatross. *Diomedia chlorhynchos* _____

140

Shearwaters, Petrels and Fulmars *(Procellariidae)*

☐ Northern Fulmar. *Fulmarus glacialis* _____

☐ Black-capped Petrel. *Pterodroma hasitata* _____

☐ Mottled Petrel. *Pterodroma inexpectata* _____

☐ Streaked Shearwater. *Calonectris leucomelas* _____

☐ Cory's Shearwater. *Calonectris diomedea* _____

☐ Pink-footed Shearwater. *Puffinus creatopus.* _____

☐ Flesh-footed Shearwater. *Puffinus carneipes* _____

☐ Greater Shearwater. *Puffinus gravis* _____

☐ Buller's Shearwater. *Puffinus bulleri* _____

☐ Sooty Shearwater. *Puffinus griseus* _____

☐ Short-tailed Shearwater. *Puffinus tenuirostris* _____

☐ Manx Shearwater. *Puffinus puffinus* _____

☐ Black-vented Shearwater. *Puffinus opisthomelas* _____

☐ Little Shearwater. *Puffinus assimilis* _____

☐ Audubon's Shearwater. *Puffinus lherminieri* _____

Storm-Petrels *(Hydrosatidae)*

☐ Wilson's Storm-Petrel. *Oceanites oceanicus* _____

☐ White-faced Storm-Petrel. *Pelagodroma marina* _____

☐ British Storm-Petrel. *Hydrobates pelagicus* _____

☐ Fork-tailed Storm-Petrel. *Oceanodroma furcata* _____

☐ Leach's Storm-Petrel. *Oceanodroma leucorhoa* _____

☐ Ashy Storm-Petrel. *Oceanodroma homochroa* _____

☐ Band-rumped Storm-Petrel. *Oceanodroma castro* _____

☐ Wedge-rumped Storm-Petrel. *Oceanodroma tethys* _____

☐ Black Storm-Petrel. *Oceanodroma melania* _____

☐ Least Storm-Petrel. *Oceanodroma microsoma* _____

Tropicbirds *(Phaethontidae)*

☐ White-tailed Tropicbird. *Phaethon lepturus* _____

☐ Red-billed Tropicbird. *Phaethon aethereus* _____

☐ Red-tailed Tropicbird. *Phaethon rubricauda* _____

Gannets and Boobies *(Sulidae)*

☐ Masked Booby. *Sula dactylatra* _____

☐ Blue-footed Booby. *Sula nebouxii* _____

☐ Brown Booby. *Sula leucogaster* _____

☐ Red-footed Booby. *Sula sula* _____

☐ Northern Gannet. *Sula bassanus* _____

Pelicans *(Pelecanidae)*

☐ American White Pelican. *Pelecanus erythrorhynchos* _____

☐ Brown Pelican. *Pelecanus occidentalis* _____

Cormorants *(Phalacrocoracidae)*

☐ Great Cormorant. *Phalacrocorax carbo* _____

☐ Double-crested
Cormorant. *Phalacrocorax auritus*   _____

☐ Olivaceous Cormorant. *Phalacrocorax
olivaceus*   _____

☐ Brandt's Cormorant. *Phalacrocorax
penicillatus*   _____

☐ Pelagic Cormorant. *Phalacrocorax
pelagicus*   _____

☐ Red-faced Cormorant. *Phalacrocorax
urile*   _____

Anhingas *(Anhingidae)*

☐ Anhinga. *Anhinga anhinga*   _____

Frigatebirds *(Fregatidae)*

☐ Magnificent Frigatebird. *Fregata
magnificens*   _____

☐ Great Frigatebird. *Fregata minor*   _____

☐ Lesser Frigatebird. *Fregata ariel*   _____

Herons *(Ardeidae)*

☐ American Bittern. *Botaurus
lentiginosus*   _____

☐ Least Bittern. *Ixobrychus exilis*   _____

☐ Great Blue Heron. *Ardea herodias*   _____

☐ Great Egret. *Casmerodius albus*   _____

☐ Chinese Egret. *Egretta eulophotes*   _____

☐ Little Egret. *Egretta garzetta*   _____

☐ Snowy Egret. *Egretta thula*   _____

☐ Little Blue Heron. *Egretta
caerulea*   _____

☐ Tricolored Heron. *Egretta tricolor*   _____

☐ Reddish Egret. *Egretta rufescens*   _____

☐ Cattle Egret. *Bubulcus ibis*   _____

☐ Green-backed Heron. *Butorides
striatus*   _____

☐ Black-crowned Night-
Heron. *Nycticorax nycticorax*   _____

☐ Yellow-crowned Night-
Heron. *Nycticorax violaceus*   _____

Ibises and Spoonbills *(Threskiornithidae)*

☐ White Ibis. *Eudocimus albus*   _____

☐ Scarlet Ibis. *Eudocimus ruber*   _____

☐ Glossy Ibis. *Plegadis falcinellus*   _____

☐ White-faced Ibis. *Plegadis chihi*   _____

☐ Roseate Spoonbill. *Ajaia ajaja*   _____

Storks *(Ciconiidae)*

☐ Jabiru. *Jabiru mycteria*   _____

☐ Wood Stork. *Mycteria americana*   _____

Flamingos *(Phoenicopteridae)*

☐ Greater Flamingo. *Phoenicopterus
ruber*   _____

Swans, Geese and Ducks *(Anatidae)*

☐ Fulvous Whistling-Duck. *Dendrocygna
bicolor*   _____

☐ Black-bellied Whistling-Duck.
Dendrocygna autumnalis   _____

☐ Tundra Swan. *Cygnus columbianus*   _____

☐ Whooper Swan. *Cygnus cygnus*   _____

☐ Trumpeter Swan. *Cygnus buccinator*   _____

☐ Mute Swan. *Cygnus olor*   _____

☐ Bean Goose. *Anser fabalis*   _____

☐ Pink-footed Goose. *Anser
brachyrhynchus*   _____

☐ Lesser White-fronted Goose. *Anser
erythropus*   _____

☐ Greater White-fronted Goose. *Anser
albifrons*   _____

☐ Snow Goose. *Chen caerulescens* _____

☐ Ross' Goose. *Chen rossii* _____

☐ Emperor Goose. *Chen canagica* _____

☐ Brant. *Branta bernicla* _____

☐ Barnacle Goose. *Branta leucopsis* _____

☐ Canada Goose. *Branta canadensis* _____

☐ Wood Duck. *Aix sponsa* _____

☐ Green-winged Teal. *Anas crecca* _____

☐ Baikal Teal. *Anas formosa* _____

☐ Falcated Teal. *Anas falcata* _____

☐ American Black Duck. *Anas rubripes* _____

☐ Mottled Duck. *Anas fulvigula* _____

☐ Mallard. *Anas platyrhynchos* _____

☐ Spot-billed Duck. *Anas poecilorhyncha* _____

☐ White-cheeked Pintail. *Anas bahamensis* _____

☐ Northern Pintail. *Anas acuta* _____

☐ Garçaney. *Anas querquedula* _____

☐ Blue-winged Teal. *Anas discors* _____

☐ Cinnamon Teal. *Anas cyanoptera* _____

☐ Northern Shoveler. *Anas clypeata* _____

☐ Gadwall. *Anas strepera* _____

☐ Eurasian Wigeon. *Anas penelope* _____

☐ American Wigeon. *Anas americana* _____

☐ Common Pochard. *Aythya ferina* _____

☐ Canvasback. *Aythya valisineria* _____

☐ Redhead. *Aythya americana* _____

☐ Ring-necked Duck. *Aythya collaris* _____

☐ Tufted Duck. *Aythya fuligula* _____

☐ Greater Scaup. *Aythya marila* _____

☐ Lesser Scaup. *Aythya affinis* _____

☐ Common Eider. *Somateria mollissima* _____

☐ King Eider. *Somateria spectabilis* _____

☐ Spectacled Eider. *Somateria fischeri* _____

☐ Steller's Eider. *Polysticta stelleri* _____

☐ Harlequin Duck. *Histrionicus histrionicus.* _____

☐ Oldsquaw. *Clangula hyemalis* _____

☐ Black Scoter. *Melanitta nigra* _____

☐ Surf Scoter. *Melanitta perspiciliata* _____

☐ White-winged Scoter. *Melanitta fusca* _____

☐ Common Goldeneye. *Bucephala clangula* _____

☐ Barrow's Goldeneye. *Bucephala islandica* _____

☐ Bufflehead. *Bucephala albeola* _____

☐ Smew. *Mergellus albellus* _____

☐ Hooded Merganser. *Lophodytes cucullatus* _____

☐ Common Merganser. *Mergus merganser* _____

☐ Red-breasted Merganser. *Mergus serrator* _____

☐ Ruddy Duck. *Oxyura jamaicensis* _____

☐ Masked Duck. *Oxyura dominica* _____

American Vultures *(Cathartidae)*

☐ Black Vulture. *Coragyps atratus* _____

☐ Turkey Vulture. *Cathartes aura* _____

☐ California Condor. *Gymnogyps californianus* _____

Kites, Hawks and Eagles *(Accipitridae)*

☐ Osprey. *Pandion haliaetus* _____

☐ Hook-billed Kite. *Chondrohierax uncinatus* _____

☐ American Swallow-tailed Kite. *Elanoides forficatus* _____

☐ Black-shouldered Kite. *Elanus caeruleus* _____

☐ Snail Kite. *Rostrhamus sociabilis* _____

☐ Mississippi Kite. *Ictinia mississippiensis* _____

☐ Bald Eagle. *Haliaeetus leucocephalus* _____

☐ White-tailed Eagle. *Haliaeetus albicilla* _____

☐ Steller's Sea-Eagle. *Haliaeetus pelagicus* _____

☐ Northern Harrier. *Circus cyaneus* _____

☐ Sharp-shinned Hawk. *Accipiter striatus* _____

☐ Cooper's Hawk. *Accipiter cooperii* _____

☐ Northern Goshawk. *Accipiter gentilis* _____

☐ Common Black-Hawk. *Buteogallus anthracinus* _____

☐ Harris' Hawk. *Parabuteo unicinctus* _____

☐ Gray Hawk. *Buteo nitidus* _____

☐ Roadside Hawk. *Buteo magnirostris* _____

☐ Red-shouldered Hawk. *Buteo lineatus* _____

☐ Broad-winged Hawk. *Buteo platypterus* _____

☐ Short-tailed Hawk. *Buteo brachyurus* _____

☐ Swainson's Hawk. *Buteo swainsoni* _____

☐ White-tailed Hawk. *Buteo albicaudatus* _____

☐ Zone-tailed Hawk. *Buteo albonotatus* _____

☐ Red-tailed Hawk. *Buteo jamaicensis* _____

☐ Ferruginous Hawk. *Buteo regalis* _____

☐ Rough-legged Hawk. *Buteo lagopus* _____

☐ Golden Eagle. *Aquila chrysaetos* _____

Falcons and Caracara *(Falconidae)*

☐ Crested Caracara. *Polyborus plancus* _____

☐ Eurasian Kestrel. *Falco tinnunculus* _____

☐ American Kestrel. *Falco sparverius* _____

☐ Merlin. *Falco columbarius* _____

☐ Aplomado Falcon. *Falco femoralis* _____

☐ Peregrine Falcon. *Falco peregrinus* _____

☐ Gyrfalcon. *Falco rusticolus* _____

☐ Prairie Falcon. *Falco mexicanus* _____

Chachalacas *(Cracidae)*

☐ Plain Chachalaca. *Ortalis vetula* _____

Grouse and Ptarmigan *(Phasianidae)*

☐ Gray Partridge. *Perdix perdix* _____

☐ Black Francolin. *Francolinus francolinus* _____

☐ Chukar. *Alectoris chukar* _____

☐ Ring-necked Pheasant. *Phasianus colchicus* _____

☐ Spruce Grouse. *Dendragapus canadensis* _____

☐ Blue Grouse. *Dendragapus obscurus* _____

☐ Willow Ptarmigan. *Lagopus lagopus* _____

☐ Rock Ptarmigan. *Lagopus mutus* _____

☐ White-tailed Ptarmigan. *Logopus leucurus* _____

☐ Ruffed Grouse. *Bonasa umbellus* _____

☐ Sage Grouse. *Centrocercus urophasianus* _____

☐ Greater Prairie-Chicken. *Tympanuchus cupido* _____

☐ Lesser Prairie-Chicken. *Tympanuchus pallidicinctus* _____

☐ Sharp-tailed Grouse. *Tympanuchus phasianellus* _____

☐ Wild Turkey. *Meleagris gallopavo* _____

☐ Montezuma Quail. *Cyrtonyx montezumae* _____

☐ Northern Bobwhite. *Colinus virginianus* _____

☐ Scaled Quail. *Callipepla squamata* _____

☐ Gambel's Quail. *Callipepla gambelii* _____

☐ California Quail. *Callipepla californica* _____

☐ Mountain Quail. *Oreortyx pictus* _____

Rails, Gallinules and Coots *(Rallidae)*

☐ Yellow Rail. *Coturnicops noveboracensis* _____

☐ Black Rail. *Laterallus jamaicensis* _____

☐ Corn Crake. *Crex crex* _____

☐ Clapper Rail. *Rallus longirostris* _____

☐ King Rail. *Rallus elegans* _____

☐ Virginia Rail. *Rallus limicola* _____

☐ Sora. *Porzana carolina* _____

☐ Paint-billed Crake. *Neocrex erythrops* _____

☐ Spotted Rail. *Pardirallus maculatus* _____

☐ Purple Gallinule. *Porphyrula martinica* _____

☐ Common Moorhen. *Gallinula chloropus* _____

☐ Eurasian Coot. *Fulica atra* _____

☐ American Coot. *Fulica americana* _____

□ Caribbean Coot. *Fulica caribaea*   _____

Limpkins *(Aramidae)*
□ *Limpkin. Aramus guarauna*   _____

Cranes *(Gruidae)*
□ *Sandhill Crane. Grus canadensis*   _____
□ *Whooping Crane. Grus americana*   _____

Thick-knees *(Burhinidae)*

□ Double-striped Thick-knee. *Burhinus
bistriatus*   _____

Plovers *(Charadriidae)*

□ Northern Lapwing. *Vanellus vanellus*   _____

□ Black-bellied Plover. *Pluvialis
squatarola*   _____

□ Greater Golden Plover. *Pluvialis
apricaria*   _____

□ Lesser Golden-Plover. *Pluvialis
dominica*   _____

□ Mongolian Plover. *Charadrius
mongolus*   _____

□ Snowy Plover. *Charadrius
alexandrinus*   _____

□ Wilson's Plover. *Charadrius wilsonia*   _____

□ Common Ringed Plover. *Charadrius
hiaticula*   _____

□ Semipalmated Plover. *Charadrius
semipalmatus*   _____

□ Piping Plover. *Charadrius melodus*   _____

□ Little Ringed Plover. *Charadrius
dubius*   _____

□ Killdeer. *Charadrius vociferus*   _____

□ Mountain Plover. *Charadrius
montanus*   _____

□ Eurasian Dotterel. *Charadrius
morinellus*   _____

Oystercatchers *(Haematopodidae)*

☐ American Oystercatcher.
Haematopus palliatus _____

☐ American Black Oystercatcher
Haematopus bachmani _____

Stilts and Avocets *(Recurvirostridae)*

☐ Black-necked Stilt. *Himantopus
mexicanus* _____

☐ American Avocet. *Recurvirostra
americana* _____

Jacanas *(Jacanidae)*

☐ Northern Jacana. *Jacana spinosa* _____

Sandpipers *(Scolopacidae)*

☐ Common Greenshank. *Tringa
nebularia* _____

☐ Greater Yellowlegs. *Tringa
melanoleuca* _____

☐ Lesser Yellowlegs. *Tringa flavipes* _____

☐ Marsh Sandpiper. *Tringa stagnatilis* _____

☐ Spotted Redshank. *Tringa erythropus* _____

☐ Wood Sandpiper. *Tringa glareola* _____

☐ Solitary Sandpiper. *Tringa solitaria* _____

☐ Willet. *Catoptrophorus semipalmatus* _____

☐ Wandering Tattler. *Heteroscelus
incanus* _____

☐ Gray-tailed Tattler. *Heteroscelus
brevipes* _____

☐ Common Sandpiper. *Actitis
hypoleucos* _____

☐ Spotted Sandpiper. *Actitis macularia* _____

☐ Terek Sandpiper. *Xenus cinereus* _____

☐ Upland Sandpiper. *Bartramia
longicauda* _____

☐ Little Curlew. *Numenius minutus* _____

☐ Eskimo Curlew. *Numenius borealis*   _____

☐ Whimbrel. *Numenius phaeopus*   _____

☐ Bristle-thighed Curlew. *Numenius tahitiensis*   _____

☐ Slender-billed Curlew. *Numenius tenuirostris*   _____

☐ Far Eastern Curlew. *Numenius madagascariensis*   _____

☐ Long-billed Curlew. *Numenius americanus*   _____

☐ Black-tailed Godwit. *Limosa limosa*   _____

☐ Hudsonian Godwit. *Limosa haemastica*   _____

☐ Bar-tailed Godwit. *Limosa lapponica*   _____

☐ Marbled Godwit. *Limosa fedoa*   _____

☐ Ruddy Turnstone. *Arenaria interpres*   _____

☐ Black Turnstone. *Arenaria melanocephala*   _____

☐ Surfbird. *Aphriza virgata*   _____

☐ Red Knot. *Calidris canutus*   _____

☐ Great Knot. *Calidris tenuirostris*   _____

☐ Sanderling. *Calidris alba*   _____

☐ Semipalmated Sandpiper. *Calidris pusilla*   _____

☐ Western Sandpiper. *Calidris mauri*   _____

☐ Rufous-necked Stint. *Calidris ruficollis*   _____

☐ Little Stint. *Calidris minuta*   _____

☐ Temminck's Stint. *Calidris temminckii*   _____

☐ Long-toed Stint. *Calidris subminuta*   _____

☐ Least Sandpiper. *Calidris minutilla*   _____

☐ White-rumped Sandpiper. *Calidrus fuscicollis*   _____

☐ Baird's Sandpiper. *Calidris bairdii*   _____

- ☐ Pectoral Sandpiper. *Calidris melanotos* _____
- ☐ Sharp-tailed Sandpiper. *Calidris acuminata* _____
- ☐ Purple Sandpiper. *Calidris maritima* _____
- ☐ Rock Sandpiper. *Calidris ptilocnemis* _____
- ☐ Dunlin. *Calidris alpina* _____
- ☐ Curlew Sandpiper. *Calidris ferruginea* _____
- ☐ Stilt Sandpiper. *Calidris himantopus* _____
- ☐ Spoonbill Sandpiper. *Eurynorhynchos pygmeus* _____
- ☐ Broad-billed Sandpiper. *Limicola falcinellus* _____
- ☐ Buff-breasted Sandpiper. *Tryngites subruficollis* _____
- ☐ Ruff. *Philomachus pugnax* _____
- ☐ Short-billed Dowitcher. *Limnodromus griseus* _____
- ☐ Long-billed Dowitcher. *Limnodromus scolopaceus* _____
- ☐ Jack Snipe. *Lymnocryptes minimus* _____
- ☐ Common Snipe. *Gallinago gallinago* _____
- ☐ Eurasian Woodcock. *Scolopax rusticola* _____
- ☐ American Woodcock. *Scolopax minor* _____
- ☐ Wilson's Phalarope. *Phalaropus tricolor* _____
- ☐ Red-necked Phalarope. *Phalaropus lobatus* _____
- ☐ Red Phalarope. *Phalaropus fulicaria* _____

Gulls, Terns, Skuas and Jaegers *(Laridae)*

- ☐ Pomarine Jaeger. *Stercorarius pomarinus* _____
- ☐ Parasitic Jaeger. *Stercorarius parasiticus* _____

☐ Long-tailed Jaeger. *Stercorarius longicaudus* _____

☐ Great Skua. *Catharacta skua* _____

☐ South Polar Skua. *Catharacta maccormicki* _____

☐ Laughing Gull. *Larus atricilla* _____

☐ Franklin's Gull. *Larus pipixcan* _____

☐ Little Gull. *Larus minutus* _____

☐ Common Black-headed Gull. *Larus ridibundus* _____

☐ Bonaparte's Gull. *Larus philadelphia* _____

☐ Heermann's Gull. *Larus heermanni* _____

☐ Band-tailed Gull. *Larus belcheri* _____

☐ Mew Gull. *Larus canus* _____

☐ Ring-billed Gull. *Larus delawarensis* _____

☐ California Gull. *Larus californicus* _____

☐ Herring Gull. *Larus argentatus* _____

☐ Thayer's Gull. *Larus thayeri* _____

☐ Iceland Gull. *Larus glaucoides* _____

☐ Lesser Black-backed Gull. *Larus fuscus* _____

☐ Slaty-backed Gull. *Larus schistisagus* _____

☐ Yellow-footed Gull. *Larus livens* _____

☐ Western Gull. *Larus occidentalis* _____

☐ Glaucous-winged Gull. *Larus glaucescens* _____

☐ Glaucous Gull. *Larus hyperboreus* _____

☐ Great Black-backed Gull. *Larus marinus* _____

☐ Black-legged Kittiwake. *Rissa tridactyla* _____

☐ Red-legged Kittiwake. *Rissa brevirostris* _____

☐ Ross' Gull. *Rhodostethia rosea* _____

☐ Sabine's Gull. *Xema sabini* _____

☐ Ivory Gull. *Pagophila eburnea* _____

☐ Gull-billed Tern. *Sterna nilotica* _____

☐ Caspian Tern. *Sterna caspia* _____

☐ Royal Tern. *Sterna maxima* _____

☐ Elegant Tern. *Sterna elegans* _____

☐ Sandwich Tern. *Sterna sandvicensis.* _____

☐ Roseate Tern. *Sterna dougallii* _____

☐ Common Tern. *Sterna hirundo* _____

☐ Arctic Tern. *Sterna paradisaea* _____

☐ Forster's Tern. *Sterna forsteri* _____

☐ Least Tern. *Sterna antillarum* _____

☐ Aleutian Tern. *Sterna aleutica* _____

☐ Bridled Tern. *Sterna anaethetus* _____

☐ Sooty Tern. *Sterna fuscata* _____

☐ White-winged Tern. *Chlidonias leucopterus* _____

☐ Black Tern. *Chlidonias niger* _____

☐ Brown Noddy. *Anous stolidus* _____

☐ Black Noddy. *Anous minutus* _____

☐ Black Skimmer. *Rynchops niger* _____

Auks and Puffins *(Alcidae)*

☐ Dovekie. *Alle alle* _____

☐ Common Murre. *Uria aalge* _____

☐ Thick-billed Murre. *Uria lomvia* _____

☐ Razorbill. *Alca torda* _____

☐ Black Guillemot. *Cepphus grylle* _____

☐ Pigeon Guillemot. *Cepphus columba* _____

☐ Marbled Murrelet. *Brachyramphus marmoratus* _____

☐ Kittlitz's Murrelet. *Brachyramphus brevirostris* _____

☐ Xantus' Murrelet. *Synthliboramphus hypoleucus* _____

☐ Craveri's Murrelet. *Synthliboramphus craveri* _____

☐ Ancient Murrelet. *Synthliboramphus antiquus* _____

☐ Cassin's Auklet. *Ptychoramphys aleuticus* _____

☐ Parakeet Auklet. *Cyclorrhynchus psittacula* _____

☐ Least Auklet. *Aethia pusilla* _____

☐ Whiskered Auklet. *Aethia pygmaea* _____

☐ Crested Auklet. *Aethia cristatella* _____

☐ Rhinoceros Auklet. *Cerorhinca monocerata* _____

☐ Tufted Puffin. *Fratercula cirrhata* _____

☐ Atlantic Puffin. *Fratercula arctica* _____

☐ Horned Puffin. *Fratercula corniculata* _____

Pigeons and Doves *(Columbidae)*

☐ Rock Dove. *Columba livia* _____

☐ Scaly-naped Pigeon. *Columba squamosa* _____

☐ White-crowned Pigeon. *Columba leucocephala* _____

☐ Red-billed Pigeon. *Columba flavirostris* _____

☐ Band-tailed Pigeon. *Columba fasciata* _____

☐ Ringed Turtle-Dove. *Streptopelia risoria* _____

☐ Spotted Dove. *Streptopelia chinensis* _____

☐ White-winged Dove. *Zenaida asiatica* _____

☐ Zenaida Dove. *Zenaida aurita* _____

☐ Mourning Dove. *Zenaida macroura* _____

☐ Inca Dove. *Columbina inca* _____

☐ Common Ground-Dove. *Columbina passerina* _____

☐ Ruddy Ground-Dove. *Columbina talpacoti* _____

☐ White-tipped Dove. *Leptotila verreauxi* _____

☐ Key West Quail-Dove. *Geotrygon chrysia* _____

☐ Ruddy Quail-Dove. *Geotrygon montana* _____

Parrots *(Psittacidae)*

☐ Budgerigar. *Melopsittacus undulatus* _____

☐ Rose-ringer Parakeet. *Psittacula krameri* _____

☐ Monk Parakeet. *Myopsitta monachus* _____

☐ Thick-billed Parrot. *Rhynchopsitta pachyrhyncha* _____

☐ Canary-winged Parakeet. *Brotogeris versicolurus* _____

☐ Red-crowned Parrot. *Amazona viridigenalis* _____

Cuckoos, Anis and Roadrunners *(Cuculidae)*

☐ Common Cuckoo. *Cuculus canorus* _____

☐ Oriental Cuckoo. *Cuculus saturatus* _____

☐ Black-billed Cuckoo. *Coccyzus erythropthalmus* _____

☐ Yellow-billed Cuckoo. *Coccyzus americanus* _____

☐ Mangrove Cuckoo. *Coccyzus minor* _____

☐ Greater Roadrunner. *Geococcyx californianus* _____

☐ Smooth-billed Ani. *Crotophaga ani* _____

☐ Groove-billed Ani. *Crotophaga sulcirostris* _____

Barn Owls *(Tytonidae)*

☐ Common Barn-Owl. *Tyto alba* _____

Owls *(Strigidae)*

☐ Oriental Scops-Owl. *Otus sunia* _____

☐ Flammulated Owl. *Otus flammeolus* _____

☐ Eastern Screech-Owl. *Otus asio* _____

☐ Western Screech-Owl. *Otus kennicottii* _____

☐ Whiskered Screech-Owl. *Otus trichopsis* _____

☐ Great Horned Owl. *Bubo virginianus* _____

☐ Snowy Owl. *Nyctea scandiaca* _____

☐ Northern Hawk-Owl. *Surnia ulula* _____

☐ Northern Pygmy-Owl. *Glaucidium gnoma* _____

☐ Ferruginous Pygmy-Owl. *Glaucidium brasilianum* _____

☐ Elf Owl. *Micrathene whitneyi* _____

☐ Burrowing Owl. *Athene cunicularia* _____

☐ Spotted Owl. *Strix occidentalis* _____

☐ Barred Owl. *Strix varia* _____

☐ Great Gray Owl. *Strix nebulosa* _____

☐ Long-eared Owl. *Asio otus* _____

☐ Short-eared Owl. *Asio flammeus* _____

☐ Boreal Owl. *Aegolius funereus* _____

☐ Northern Saw-whet Owl. *Aegolius acadicus* _____

Nightjars *(Caprimulgidae)*

☐ Lesser Nighthawk. *Chordeiles acutipennis* _____

☐ Common Nighthawk. *Chordeiles minor* _____

- Antillean Nighthawk. *Chordeiles gundlachii* _____
- Common Pauraque. *Nyctidromus albicollis* _____
- Common Poorwill. *Phalaenoptilus nuttallii* _____
- Chuck-will's-widow. *Caprimulgus carolinensis* _____
- Buff-collared Nightjar. *Caprimulgus ridgwayi* _____
- Whip-poor-will. *Caprimulgus vociferus* _____
- Jungle Nightjar. *Caprimulgus indicus* _____

Swifts *(Apodidae)*

- Black Swift. *Cypseloides niger.* _____
- White-collared Swift. *Streptoprocne zonaris* _____
- Chimney Swift. *Chaetura pelagica* _____
- Vaux's Swift. *Chaetura vauxi* _____
- White-throated Needletail. *Hirundapus caudacutus* _____
- Common Swift. *Apus apus* _____
- Fork-tailed Swift. *Apus pacificus* _____
- White-throated Swift. *Aeronautes saxatalis* _____
- Antillean Palm Swift. *Tachornis phoenicobia* _____

Hummingbirds *(Trochilidae)*

- Green Violet-ear. *Colibri thalassinus* _____
- Broad-billed Hummingbird. *Cynanthus latirostris* _____
- White-eared Hummingbird. *Hylocharis leucotis* _____
- Berylline Hummingbird. *Amazilia beryllina* _____

☐ Rufous-tailed Hummingbird. *Amazilia tzacatl*

_____

☐ Buff-bellied Hummingbird. *Amazilia yucatanensis*

_____

☐ Violet-crowned Hummingbird. *Amazilia violiceps*

_____

☐ Blue-throated Hummingbird. *Lampornis clemenciae*

_____

☐ Magnificent Hummingbird. *Eugenes fulgens*

_____

☐ Plain-capped Starthroat. *Heliomaster constantii*

_____

☐ Bahama Woodstar. *Calliphlox evelynae*

_____

☐ Lucifer Hummingbird. *Calothorax lucifer*

_____

☐ Ruby-throated Hummingbird. *Archilochus colubris*

_____

☐ Black-chinned Hummingbird. *Archilochus alexandri*

_____

☐ Anna's Hummingbird. *Calypte anna*   _____

☐ Costa's Hummingbird. *Calypte costae* _____

☐ Calliope Hummingbird. *Stellula calliope*

_____

☐ Bumblebee Hummingbird. *Atthis heloisa*

_____

☐ Broad-tailed Hummingbird. *Selasphorus platycercus*

_____

☐ Rufous Hummingbird. *Selasphorus rufus*

_____

☐ Allen's Hummingbird. *Selasphorus sasin*

_____

Trogons *(Trogonidae)*

☐ Elegant Trogon. *Trogon elegans* _____

☐ Eared Trogon. *Euptilotus neoxenus* _____

Hoopoes *(Upupidae)*

☐ Hoopoe. *Upupa epops* _____

Kingfishers *(Alcedinidae)*

☐ Ringed Kingfisher. *Ceryle torquata* _____

☐ Belted Kingfisher. *Ceryle alcyon* _____

☐ Green Kingfisher. *Chloroceryle americana* _____

Woodpeckers *(Picidae)*

☐ Eurasian Wryneck. *Jynx torquilla* _____

☐ Lewis' Woodpecker. *Melanerpes lewis* _____

☐ Red-headed Woodpecker. *Melanerpes erythrocephalus* _____

☐ Acorn Woodpecker. *Melanerpes formicivorus* _____

☐ Gila Woodpecker. *Melanerpes uropygialis* _____

☐ Golden-fronted Woodpecker. *Melanerpes aurifrons* _____

☐ Red-bellied Woodpecker. *Melanerpes carolinus* _____

☐ Yellow-bellied Sapsucker. *Sphyrapicus varius* _____

☐ Red-breasted Sapsucker. *Sphyrapicus ruber* _____

☐ Williamson's Sapsucker. *Sphyrapicus thyroideus* _____

☐ Ladder-backed Woodpecker *Picoides scalaris* _____

☐ Nuttall's Woodpecker. *Picoides nuttallii* _____

☐ Downy Woodpecker. *Picoides
pubescens* _____

☐ Hairy Woodpecker. *Picoides villosus* _____

☐ Strickland's Woodpecker. *Picoides
stricklandi* _____

☐ Red-cockaded Woodpecker. *Picoides
borealis* _____

☐ White-headed Woodpecker. *Picoides
albolarvatus* _____

☐ Three-toed Woodpecker. *Picoides
tridactylus* _____

☐ Black-backed Woodpecker. *Picoides
arcticus* _____

☐ Northern Flicker. *Colaptes auratus* _____

☐ Pileated Woodpecker. *Dryocopus
pileatus* _____

☐ Ivory-billed Woodpecker.
Campephilus principalis _____

Tyrant Flycatchers *(Tyrannidae)*

☐ Northern Beardless-Tyrannulet.
Camptostoma imberbe _____

☐ Olive-sided Flycatcher. *Contopus
borealis* _____

☐ Greater Pewee. *Contopus pertinax* _____

☐ Western Wood-Pewee. *Contopus
sordidulus* _____

☐ Eastern Wood-Pewee. *Contopus
virens* _____

☐ Yellow-bellied Flycatcher. *Empidonax
flaviventris* _____

☐ Acadian Flycatcher. *Empidonax
virescens* _____

☐ Alder Flycatcher. *Empidonax alnorum* _____

☐ Willow Flycatcher. *Empidonax traillii* _____

☐ Least Flycatcher. *Empidonax minimus* _____

☐ Hammond's Flycatcher. *Empidonax hammondii*

    _____

☐ Dusky Flycatcher. *Empidonax oberholseri*

    _____

☐ Gray Flycatcher. *Empidonax wrightii*   _____

☐ Western Flycatcher. *Empidonax difficilis*

    _____

☐ Buff-breasted Flycatcher. *Empidonax fulvifrons*

    _____

☐ Black Phoebe. *Sayornis nigricans*   _____

☐ Eastern Phoebe. *Sayornis phoebe*   _____

☐ Say's Phoebe. *Sayornis saya*   _____

☐ Vermilion Flycatcher. *Pyrocephalus rubinus*

    _____

☐ Dusky-capped Flycathcer. *Myiarchus tuberculifer*

    _____

☐ Ash-throated Flycatcher. *Myiarchus cinerascens*

    _____

☐ Great Crested Flycatcher. *Miarchus crinitus*

    _____

☐ Brown-crested Flycatcher. *Miarchus tyrannulus*

    _____

☐ Great Kiskadee. *Pitangus sulphuratus*   _____

☐ La Sagra's Flycatcher. *Myiarchus sagrae*

    _____

☐ Sulphur-bellied Flycatcher. *Myiodynastes luteiventris*

    _____

☐ Variegated Flycatcher. *Empidonomus varius*

    _____

☐ Tropical Kingbird. *Tyrannus melancholicus*

    _____

☐ Couch's Kingbird. *Tyrannus couchii*   _____

☐ Cassin's Kingbird. *Tyrannus vociferans*

    _____

☐ Thick-billed Kingbird. *Tyrannus crassirostris*

    _____

☐ Western Kingbird. *Tyrannus verticalis* _____

☐ Eastern Kingbird. *Tyrannus tyrannus* _____

☐ Gray Kingbird. *Tyrannus dominicensis* _____

☐ Loggerhead Kingbird. *Tyrannus caudifasciatus* _____

☐ Scissor-tailed Flycatcher. *Tyrannus forficatus* _____

☐ Fork-tailed Flycatcher. *Tyrannus savana* _____

☐ Rose-throated Becard. *Pachyramphus aglaiae* _____

Larks *(Alaudidae)*

☐ Eurasian Skylark. *Alauda arvensis* _____

☐ Horned Lark. *Eremophila alpestris* _____

Swallows *(Hirundinidae)*

☐ Purple Martin. *Progne subis* _____

☐ Cuban Martin. *Progne cryptoleuca* _____

☐ Gray-breasted Martin. *Progne chalybea* _____

☐ Southern Martin. *Progne elegans* _____

☐ Tree Swallow. *Tachycineta bicolor* _____

☐ Violet-green Swallow. *Tachycineta thalassina* _____

☐ Bahama Swallow. *Tachycineta cyaneoviridis* _____

☐ Northern Rough-winged Swallow. *Stelgidopteryx serripennis* _____

☐ Bank Swallow. *Riparia riparia* _____

☐ Cliff Swallow. *Hirundo pyrrhonota* _____

☐ Cave Swallow. *Hirundo fulva* _____

☐ Barn Swallow. *Hirundo rustica* _____

☐ Common House-Martin. *Delichon urbica* _____

Jays, Crows, Magpies and Ravens *(Corvidae)*

☐ Gray Jay. *Perisoreus canadensis* _____

☐ Steller's Jay. *Cyanocitta stelleri* _____

☐ Blue Jay. *Cyanocitta cristata* _____

☐ Green Jay. *Cyanocorax yncas* _____

☐ Brown Jay. *Cyanocorax morio* _____

☐ Scrub Jay. *Aphelocoma coerulescens* _____

☐ Gray-breasted Jay. *Aphelocoma ultramarina* _____

☐ Pinyon Jay. *Gymnorhinus cyanocephalus* _____

☐ Clark's Nutcracker. *Nucifraga columbiana* _____

☐ Black-billed Magpie. *Pica pica* _____

☐ Yellow-billed Magpie. *Pica nuttalli* _____

☐ American Crow. *Corvus brachyrhynchos* _____

☐ Northwestern Crow. *Corvus caurinus* _____

☐ Mexican Crow. *Corvus imparatus* _____

☐ Fish Crow. *Corvus ossifragus* _____

☐ Chihuahuan Raven. *Corvus cryptoleucus* _____

☐ Common Raven. *Corvus corax* _____

Titmice and Chickadees *(Paridae)*

☐ Black-capped Chickadee. *Parus atricapillus* _____

☐ Carolina Chickadee. *Parus carclinensis* _____

☐ Mexican Chickadee. *Parus sclateri* _____

☐ Mountain Chickadee. *Parus gambeli* _____

☐ Siberian Tit. *Parus cinctus* _____

☐ Boreal Chickadee. *Parus hudsonicus* _____

☐ Chestnut-backed Chickadee. *Parus rufescens* _____

☐ Bridled Titmouse. *Parus wollweberi* _____

☐ Plain Titmouse. *Parus inornatus* _____

☐ Tufted Titmouse. *Parus bicolor* _____

Verdins *(Remizidae)*

☐ Verdin. *Auriparus flaviceps* _____

Bushtits *(Aegithalidae)*

☐ Bushtit. *Psaltriparus minimus* _____

Nuthatches *(Sittidae)*

☐ Red-breasted Nuthatch. *Sitta canadensis* _____

☐ White-breasted Nuthatch. *Sita carolinensis* _____

☐ Pygmy Nuthatch. *Sitta pygmaea* _____

☐ Brown-headed Nuthatch. *Sitta pusilla* _____

Creepers *(Certhiidae)*

☐ Brown Creeper. *Certhia americana* _____

Bulbuls *(Pycnonotidae)*

☐ Red-whiskered Bulbul. *Pycnonotus jocosus* _____

Wrens *(Troglodytidae)*

☐ Cactus Wren. *Campylorhynchus brunneicapillus* _____

☐ Rock Wren. *Salpinctes obsoletus* _____

☐ Canyon Wren. *Catherpes mexicanus* _____

☐ Carolina Wren. *Thryothorus ludovicianus* _____

☐ Bewick's Wren. *Thryomanes bewickii* _____

☐ House Wren. *Troglodytes aedon* _____

☐ Winter Wren. *Troglodytes troglodytes* _____

☐ Sedge Wren. *Cistothorus platensis* _____

☐ Marsh Wren. *Cistothorus palustris* _____

Dippers *(Cinclidae)*

☐ American Dipper. *Cinclus mexicanus* _____

Thrushers, Kinglets and Gnatcatchers *(Muscicapidaes)*

☐ Middendorf's Grasshopper
Warbler. *Locustella ochotensis* _____

☐ Wcod Warbler. *Phylloscopus sibilatrix* _____

☐ Dusky Warbler. *Phylloscopus fuscatus* _____

☐ Arctic Warbler. *Phylloscopus
borealis* _____

☐ Golden-crowned Kinglet. *Regulus
satrapa* _____

☐ Ruby-crowned Kinglet. *Regulus
calendula* _____

☐ Blue-gray Gnatcatcher. *Polioptila
caerulea* _____

☐ Black-tailed Gnatcatcher. *Polioptila
melanura* _____

☐ Black-capped Gnatcatcher. *Polioptila
nigriceps* _____

☐ Red-breasted Flycatcher. *Ficedula
parva* _____

☐ Siberian Flycatcher. *Muscicapa
sibirica* _____

☐ Gray-spotted Flycatcher. *Muscicapa
griseisticta* _____

☐ Siberian Rubythroat. *Luscinia calliope* _____

☐ Bluethroat. *Luscinia svecica* _____

☐ Northern Wheatear. *Oenanthe
cenanthe* _____

☐ Eastern Bluebird. *Sialia sialis* _____

☐ Western Bluebird. *Sialia mexicana* _____

☐ Mountain Bluebird. *Sialia currucoides* _____

☐ Townsend's Solitaire. *Myadestes
townsendi* _____

☐ Veery. *Catharus fuscescens* _____

☐ Gray-cheeked Thrush. *Catharus minimus* _____

☐ Swainson's Thrush. *Catharus ustulatus* _____

☐ Hermit Thrush. *Catharus guttatus* _____

☐ Wood Thrush. *Hylocichla mustelina* _____

☐ Eye-browed Thrush. *Turdus obscurus* _____

☐ Dusky Thrush. *Turdus naumanni* _____

☐ Fieldfare. *Turdus pilaris* _____

☐ Clay-colored Robin. *Turdus grayi* _____

☐ Rufous-backed Robin. *Turdus rufopalliatus* _____

☐ American Robin. *Turdus migratorius* _____

☐ Varied Thrush. *Ixoreus naevius* _____

☐ Aztec Thrush. *Ridgwayia pinicola* _____

☐ Wrentit. *Chamaea fasciata* _____

Mockingbirds, Thrashers, and Catbirds *(Mimidae)*

☐ Gray Catbird. *Dumetella carolinensis* _____

☐ Northern Mockingbird. *Mimus polyglottos* _____

☐ Bahama Mockingbird. *Mimus gundlachii* _____

☐ Sage Thrasher. *Oreoscoptes montanus* _____

☐ Brown Thrasher. *Toxostoma rufum* _____

☐ Long-billed Thrasher. *Toxostoma longirostre* _____

☐ Bendire's Thrasher. *Toxostoma bendirei* _____

☐ Curve-billed Thrasher. *Toxostoma curvirostre* _____

☐ California Thrasher. *Toxostoma redivivum* _____

☐ Crissal Thrasher. *Toxostoma dorsale* _____

☐ Le Conte's Thrasher. *Toxostoma lecontei* _____

Accentors *(Prunellidae)*

☐ Siberian Accentor. *Prunella montanella* _____

Pipits and Wagtails *(Motacillidae)*

☐ Yellow Wagtail. *Motacilla flava* _____

☐ Gray Wagtail. *Motacilla cinerea* _____

☐ White Wagtail. *Motacilla alba* _____

☐ Black-backed Wagtail. *Motacilla lugens* _____

☐ Brown Tree-Pipit. *Anthus trivialis* _____

☐ Olive Tree-Pipit. *Anthus hodgsoni* _____

☐ Pechora Pipit. *Anthus gustavi* _____

☐ Red-throated Pipit. *Anthus cervinus* _____

☐ Water Pipit. *Anthus spinoletta* _____

☐ Sprague's Pipit. *Anthus spragueii* _____

Waxwings *(Bombycillidae)*

☐ Bohemian Waxwing. *Bombycilla garrulus* _____

☐ Cedar Waxwing. *Bombycilla cedrorum* _____

Phainopeplas (or Silky Flycatchers) *(Ptilogonatidae)*

☐ Phainopepla. *Phainopepla nitens* _____

Shrikes *(Laniidae)*

☐ Brown Shrike. *Lanius cristatus* _____

☐ Northern Shrike. *Lanius excubitor* _____

☐ Loggerhead Shrike. *Lanius ludovicianus* _____

Starlings *(Sturnidae)*

☐ European Starling. *Sturnus vulgaris* _____

☐ Crested Myna. *Acridotheres cristatellus* _____

Vireos *(Vireonidae)*

☐ White-eyed Vireo. *Vireo griseus* _____

☐ Bell's Vireo. *Vireo bellii* _____

☐ Black-capped Vireo. *Vireo atricapillus* _____

☐ Gray Vireo. *Vireo vicinior* _____

☐ Solitary Vireo. *Vireo solitarius* _____

☐ Yellow-throated Vireo. *Vireo flavifrons* _____

☐ Hutton's Vireo. *Vireo huttoni* _____

☐ Warbling Vireo. *Vireo gilvus* _____

☐ Philadelphia Vireo. *Vireo philadelphicus* _____

☐ Red-eyed Vireo. *Vireo olivaceus* _____

☐ Black-whiskered Vireo. *Vireo altiloquus* _____

Wood Warblers, Tanagers, Sparrows, Blackbirds and Orioles *(Emberizidae)*

☐ Bachman's Warbler. *Vermivora bachmanii* _____

☐ Blue-winged Warbler. *Vermivora pinus* _____

☐ Golden-winged Warbler. *Vermivora chrysoptera* _____

☐ Tennessee Warbler. *Vermivora peregrina* _____

☐ Orange-crowned Warbler. *Vermivora celata* _____

☐ Nashville Warbler. *Vermivora ruficapilla* _____

☐ Virginia's Warbler. *Vermivora virginiae* _____

☐ Crescent-chested Warbler. *Vermivora superciliosa* _____

☐ Colima Warbler. *Vermivora crissalis* _____

☐ Lucy's Warbler. *Vermivora luciae* _____

☐ Northern Parula. *Parula americana* _____

☐ Tropical Parula. *Parula pitiayumi* _____

☐ Yellow Warbler. *Dendroica petechia* _____

☐ Chestnut-sided Warbler. *Dendroica pensylvanica* _____

☐ Magnolia Warbler. *Dendroica magnolia* _____

☐ Cape May Warbler. *Dendroica tigrina* _____

☐ Black-throated Blue Warbler. *Dendroica caerulescens* _____

☐ Yellow-rumped Warbler. *Dendroica coronata* _____

☐ Black-throated Gray Warbler. *Dendroica nigrescens* _____

☐ Townsend's Warbler. *Dendroica townsendi* _____

☐ Hermit Warbler. *Dendroica occidentalis* _____

☐ Black-throated Green Warbler *Dendroica virens* _____

☐ Golden-cheeked Warbler. *Dendroica chrysoparia* _____

☐ Blackburnian Warbler. *Dendroica fusca* _____

☐ Yellow-throated Warbler. *Dendroica dominica* _____

☐ Grace's Warbler. *Dendroica graciae* _____

☐ Pine Warbler. *Dendroica pinus* _____

☐ Kirtland's Warbler. *Dendroica kirtlandii* _____

☐ Prairie Warbler. *Dendroica discolor* _____

☐ Palm Warbler. *Dendroica palmarum* _____

☐ Bay-breasted Warbler. *Dendroica castanea* _____

☐ Blackpoll Warbler. *Dendroica striata* _____

☐ Cerulean Warbler. *Dendroica cerulea* _____

☐ Black-and-white Warbler. *Mniotilta varia* _____

☐ American Redstart. *Setophaga ruticilla* _____

☐ Prothonotary Warbler. *Protonotaria citrea* _____

☐ Worm-eating Warbler. *Helmitheros vermivorus* _____

☐ Swainson's Warbler. *Limnothlypis swainsonii* _____

☐ Ovenbird. *Seiurus aurocapillus* _____

☐ Northern Waterthrush. *Seiurus noveboracensis* _____

☐ Louisiana Waterthrush. *Seiurus motacilla* _____

☐ Kentucky Warbler. *Oporornis formosus* _____

☐ Connecticut Warbler. *Oporornis agilis* _____

☐ Mourning Warbler. *Oporornis philadelphia* _____

☐ MacGillivray's Warbler. *Oporornis tolmiei* _____

☐ Common Yellowthroat. *Geothlypis trichas* _____

☐ Gray-crowned Yellowthroat. *Geothlypis poliocephala* _____

☐ Hooded Warbler. *Wilsonia citrina* _____

☐ Wilson's Warbler. *Wilsonia pusilla* _____

☐ Canada Warbler. *Wilsonia canadensis* _____

☐ Red-faced Warbler. *Cardellina rubrifrons* _____

☐ Painted Redstart. *Myioborus pictus* _____

☐ Slate-throated Redstart. *Myiaborus miniatus* _____

☐ Fan-tailed Warbler. *Euthlypis lachrymosa* _____

☐ Golden-crowned Warbler. *Basileuterus culicivorus* _____

☐ Rufous-capped Warbler. *Basileuterus rufifrons* _____

☐ Yellow-breasted Chat. *Icteria virens* _____

☐ Olive Warbler. *Peucedramus taeniatus* _____

☐ Bananaquit. *Coereba flaveola* _____

☐ Stripe-headed Tanager. *Spindalis zena* _____

☐ Hepatic Tanager. *Piranga flava* _____

☐ Summer Tanager. *Piranga rubra* _____

☐ Scarlet Tanager. *Piranga olivacea* _____

☐ Western Tanager. *Piranga ludoviciana* _____

☐ Crimson-collared Grosbeak. *Rhodothraupus celaeno* _____

☐ Northern Cardinal. *Cardinalis cardinalis* _____

☐ Pyrrhuloxia. *Cardinalis sinuatus* _____

☐ Yellow Grosbeak. *Pheucticus chrysopeplus* _____

☐ Rose-breasted Grosbeak. *Pheucticus ludovicianus* _____

☐ Black-headed Grosbeak. *Pheucticus melanocephalus* _____

☐ Blue Bunting. *Cyanocompsa parellina* _____

☐ Blue Grosbeak. *Guiraca caerulea* _____

☐ Lazuli Bunting. *Passerina amoena* _____

☐ Indigo Bunting. *Passerina cyanea* _____

☐ Varied Bunting. *Passerina versicolor* _____

☐ Painted Bunting. *Passerina ciris* _____

☐ Dickcissel. *Spiza americana* _____

☐ Olive Sparrow. *Arremonops rufivirgatus* _____

☐ Green-tailed Towhee. *Pipilo chlorurus* _____

☐ Rufous-sided Towhee. *Pipilo erythrophthalmus* _____

☐ Brown Towhee. *Pipilo fuscus* _____

☐ Abert's Towhee. *Pipilo aberti* _____

☐ White-collared Seedeater. *Sporophila torqueola* _____

☐ Black-faced Grassquit. *Tiaris bicolor* _____

☐ Bachman's Sparrow. *Aimophila aestivalis* _____

☐ Botteri's Sparrow. *Aimophila botterii* _____

☐ Cassin's Sparrow. *Aimophila cassinii* _____

☐ Rufous-winged Sparrow. *Aimophila carpalis* _____

☐ Rufous-crowned Sparrow. *Aimophila ruficeps* _____

☐ American Tree Sparrow. *Spizella arborea* _____

☐ Chipping Sparrow. *Spizella passerina* _____

☐ Clay-colored Sparrow. *Spizella pallida* _____

☐ Brewer's Sparrow. *Spizella breweri* _____

☐ Field Sparrow. *Spizella pusilla* _____

☐ Worthen's Sparrow. *Spizella wortheni* _____

☐ Black-chinned Sparrow. *Spizella atrogularis* _____

☐ Vesper Sparrow. *Pooecetes gramineus* _____

☐ Lark Sparrow. *Chondestes grammacus* _____

☐ Black-throated Sparrow. *Amphispiza bilineata* _____

☐ Sage Sparrow. *Amphispiza belli* _____

☐ Five-striped Sparrow. *Amphispiza quinquestriata* _____

☐ Lark Bunting. *Calamospiza melanocorys* _____

☐ Savannah Sparrow. *Passerculus sandwichensis* _____

☐ Baird's Sparrow. *Ammodramus bairdii* _____

☐ Grasshopper Sparrow. *Ammodramus savannarum* _____

☐ Henslow's Sparrow. *Ammodramus henslowii* _____

☐ Le Conte's Sparrow. *Ammodramus leconteii* _____

☐ Sharp-tailed Sparrow. *Ammodramus caudacutus* _____

☐ Seaside Sparrow. *Ammodramus maritimus* _____

☐ Fox Sparrow. *Passerella iliaca* _____

☐ Song Sparrow. *Melospiza melodia* _____

☐ Lincoln's Sparrow. *Melospiza lincolnii* _____

☐ Swamp Sparrow. *Melospiza georgiana* _____

☐ White-throated Sparrow. *Zonotrichia albicollis* _____

☐ Golden-crowned Sparrow. *Zonotrichia atricapilla* _____

☐ White-crowned Sparrow. *Zonotrichia leucophrys* _____

☐ Harris' Sparrow. *Zonotrichia querula* _____

☐ Dark-eyed Junco. *Junco hyemalis* _____

☐ *Yellow-eyed Junco. Junco phaeonotus* _____

☐ McCown's Longspur. *Calcarius mccownii* _____

☐ Lapland Longspur. *Calcarius lapponicus* _____

☐ Smith's Longspur. *Calcarius pictus* _____

☐ Chestnut-collared Longspur.
Calcarius ornatus _____

☐ Little Bunting. *Emberiza pusilla* _____

☐ Rustic Bunting. *Emberiza rustica* _____

☐ Pallas' Reed-Bunting. *Emberiza pallasi* _____

☐ Common Reed-Bunting. *Emberiza schoeniclus* _____

☐ Snow Bunting. *Plectrophenax nivalis* _____

☐ McKay's Bunting. *Plectrophenax hyperboreus* _____

☐ Bobolink. *Dolichonyx oryzivorus* _____

☐ Red-winged Blackbird. *Agelaius phoeniceus* _____

☐ Tricolored Blackbird. *Agelaius tricolor* _____

☐ Tawny-shouldered Blackbird. *Agelaius humeralis* _____

☐ Eastern Meadowlark. *Sturnella magna* _____

☐ Western Meadowlark. *Sturnella neglecta* _____

☐ Yellow-headed Blackbird.
Xanthocephalus xanthocephalus _____

☐ Rusty Blackbird. *Euphagus carolinus* _____

☐ Brewer's Blackbird. *Euphagus cyanocephalus* _____

☐ Great-tailed Grackle. *Quiscalus mexicanus* _____

☐ Boat-tailed Grackle. *Quiscalus major* _____

☐ Common Grackle. *Quiscalus quiscula* _____

☐ Bronzed Cowbird. *Molothrus aeneus* _____

☐ Brown-headed Cowbird. *Molothrus ater* _____

☐ Black-vented Oriole. *Icterus wagleri* _____

☐ Orchard Oriole. *Icterus spurius* _____

☐ Hooded Oriole. *Icterus cucullatus* _____

☐ Streak-backed Oriole. *Icterus pustulatus* _____

☐ Spot-breasted Oriole. *Icterus pectoralis* _____

☐ Altamira Oriole. *Icterus gularis* _____

☐ Audubon's Oriole. *Icterus graduacauda* _____

☐ Northern Oriole. *Icterus galbula* _____

☐ Scott's Oriole. *Icterus parisorum* _____

Finches *(Fringillidae)*

☐ Common Chaffinch. *Fringilla coelebs* _____

☐ Brambling. *Fringilla montifringilla* _____

☐ Rosy Finch. *Leucosticte arctoa* _____

☐ Pine Grosbeak. *Pinicola enucleator* _____

☐ Common Rosefinch. *Carpodacus erythrinus* _____

☐ Purple Finch. *Carpodacus purpureus* _____

☐ Cassin's Finch. *Carpodacus cassinii* _____

☐ House Finch. *Carpodacus mexicanus* _____

☐ Red Crossbill. *Loxia curvirostra* _____

☐ White-winged Crossbill. *Loxia leucoptera* _____

☐ Common Redpoll. *Carduelis flammea* _____

☐ Hoary Redpoll. *Carduelis hornemanni* _____

☐ Pine Siskin. *Carduelis pinus* _____

☐ Lesser Goldfinch. *Carduelis psaltria* _____

☐ Lawrence's Goldfinch. *Carduelis lawrencei* _____

☐ American Goldfinch. *Carduelis tristis* _____

☐ European Goldfinch. *Carduelis carduelis* _____

☐ Eurasian Bullfinch. *Pyrrhula pyrrhula* _____

☐ Evening Grosbeak. *Coccothraustes vespertinus*
_____

☐ Hawfinch. *Coccothraustes coccothraustes*
_____

Weavers *(Passeridae)*

☐ House Sparrow. *Passer domesticus*   _____

☐ Eurasian Tree Sparrow. *Passer montanus*
_____

9406
9143